Conflict across
the Strait

DEDICATION

This book is dedicated to the Dover Branch of the Royal Artillery Association and to the memory of those coast defenders serving in the navy, army and air force who have given their lives in the course of history in defence of the towns of South East England and in the waters of the Dover Strait.

FOREWORD

By Brigadier J. H. W. G. Richards, O.B.E., D.L., (Rtd.), (former Commanding Officer, 540 Coast Regiment, R.A., Dover).

Anyone who has had the privilege and pleasure of serving with the Coast Artillery at any time or place, as I was lucky enough to do, will find this a most interesting book to read.

The author tells his story largely from personal experiences, and records the history of the *Conflict across the Strait,* a written record which is long overdue.

The Dover defences have for centuries been the front line of home defence, and never has this been more true than during Hitler's war at which time Dover was continually reported in the press as 'Hell Fire Corner'.

I recommend this book as an interesting story to both military and civilian readers. There is a large number of people, I imagine, who like myself have admired, and been thankful to see, the White Cliffs of Dover when returning to this country.

Huntingdon.   J. H. Richards.

Conflict across the Strait

A Battery Commander's Story of Kent's Defences 1939-45

Colonel B. E. Arnold T.D.

Crabwell Publications/Buckland Publications Ltd.
2 The Ridgeway, River, Dover.

ISBN 0-906124-06-9

Cover designed by David Gates

Published jointly by Crabwell Publications
and Buckland Publications Ltd., 1982

Printed by Buckland Press Ltd., Barwick Road, Dover
and 125 High Holborn, London WC1

Contents

*The Cinque Ports Volunteer
Artillery had for centuries prepared
to defend this vital coastline.*

*Dover's coat of arms, the shield
bearing the Cinque Ports insignia,
the other two details are taken from
the town's common seal which dates
from the days of Edward I.*

1 In the beginning . . .

Before relating the story of the fight for survival in the narrow waters of the Strait of Dover, it would be well for the reader to have some brief outline of the long history of the impressed Dovorians and the local volunteer units, whose responsibility it has always been through the centuries, to defend the Town and Cinque Port of Dover.

The threat of invasion at the end of the 18th century was in many ways similar to the threat of invasion in 1941. The enemy was on our doorstep but 21 miles away, and we were half ready and less than half armed. Martello towers and similar forms of defence were hastily being built to face Napoleon, and in 1940, guns were being borrowed by the Coast Artillery and erected round the invasion coast for the same purpose, to repel an invader. The full detailed history of Coast Artillery is set out in a book *History of Coast Artillery* by Colonel K. W. Maurice-Jones. I have attempted to give an outline of the Dover defences, the Dover units, and the life and times of the men who manned those defences.

There is no doubt whatsoever, that even before the invention of gunpowder, there have been Dover defenders. Men, first armed with flint axes, bows and arrows, pikes and a diversity of strange weapons have positioned themselves on the cliffs and areas surrounding the port, defending their side of the moat, whose dividing waters separate Britain from Europe and the traditional enemies, the French, the Dutch, the Germans and even the Romans. Early records show that 'traynes of artillery' were formed and controlled by a Master Gunner in Dover Castle. He had some 47 assistants, known then as matrosses or gunners mates. In time of war or threat of war, the Cinque Ports volunteers were assembled and trained by these experts, the forerunners of the present day Instructor Gunners, and eventually became the founders of the modern Territorial Army. A Master Gunner, who lived in the time of Henry VIII, wrote a very interesting book about these 'traynes of artillery' and his book still exists and can be read today.

Evidence that the port was regarded as important can be found as far back as the Roman invasion. Recent excavations in the town, of the very highest importance, show the rank and stature of the Romans who took up their residence here. The Romans built two lighthouses on the cliffs each side of the port, virtually on the site of an old Icenic camp, to guide their galleys across the Strait from Gaul. One, the Pharos, still stands within the walls of Dover Castle, and is a well known landmark. It was originally 80 feet high and fires were kept burning on its summit, so that it could easily be seen from the cliffs of France.

Many English and Norman kings have had a hand in building Dover Castle. The Roman fortification, the Roman Oval, as it is now called, was later fortified by the Saxons, and after the Battle of Hastings, the Normans' next prime task was the capture of the town of Dover and its fortifications. To Henry II must be attributed the Castle as it stands today, and it cost him no less than £7000, nearly three-quarters of his annual income, but it was finally completed by King John.

In 1216, the castle was attacked by the French under the command of Louis, and mention is now first made of a new and frightful instrument of war, the Malvoisin, or bad neighbour, sent by Phillip of France to his son, to assist him in the siege of Dover. This 'piece of artillerie' did not avail the attacking troops very much, as the castle was defended obstinately and very bravely by one of its most outstanding commanders, Hubert de Burgh. Although the town was burnt, the castle never surrendered. This famous garrison commander, a year later, in 1217 was faced with another invasion and channel action, when Eustace le Moire, or Eustace the Monk, a French renegade priest, led 80 ships, containing a large number of French knights, across the channel to attack the port. They were met by Hubert de Burgh, who commanded 40 English ships. He surprised the French by sailing past them as if bent on a raid on Calais. However, once past, the English ships turned and attacked the French in the rear, sinking a large number and scattering the remainder. The French flagship was boarded and Eustace the Monk captured and beheaded. His head was displayed from the walls of Canterbury as evidence to those who would bring devastation to Dover.

However history tells us that the French returned again in 1295 and although they failed to capture the castle they burnt the town of Dover to the ground.

The task of Dover as a principal Cinque Port, was to supply the king's navy with men and ships in return for certain legal privileges. Historians believe that as long ago as Edward the Confessor, this agreement came into existence. Dover's contribution was 20 ships for fifteen days per annum, each ship to have a crew of twenty men and a boy.

The town has been associated with many famous names and epochs. Richard Coeur de Lion departed from the port in 1189 on his first crusade and it is said that the Knights Templar encamped just outside the town later giving their name to the village on the outskirts, Temple Ewell, and the hills on which they camped are still known today as the Templar hills. Henry V landed in Dover after his triumph on the field of Agincourt, but later in 1422, his funeral cortege, with a vast procession of knights and over 500 men at arms as well as a great company, dressed in white and carrying wax torches, landed at the port and slowly made its way through the town along the Canterbury road to Rochester and London. King James of Scotland was the chief mourner. Edward IV gathered 500 ships off the port to form an expedition to aid Charles of Burgundy. In 1522 Henry VIII stayed at the castle and then boarded the

The Roman Pharos at Dover Castle.

The Knights Templars Preceptory at Swingfield, near Dover.

The White Cliffs of Dover.

famous ship, 'Great Harry' to commence his journey to the conference now known as 'The Field of the Cloth of Gold'. Queen Elizabeth also visited the port in great pomp and circumstance. Many other epics are also associated with Dover. Queen Henrietta Maria sadly parted from her husband, Charles I, on her way to Holland to escape the men of Cromwell, whose troops by a trick and the aid of a Cromwellian sympathiser, whom we would now call a fifth columnist, surprised the royalist troops holding the castle and captured it. On the restoration of the monarchy, Charles II landed at Dover to be received by General Monk.

Further channel action is recorded when the Dutch fleet, consisting of 42 ships and commanded by Admiral Maarten Tromp, took refuge under the lee of South Foreland, and later in the Dover roads, where they exchanged some shots with the defenders then garrisoned in the castle. They sailed from Dover on 17th May, 1652, and two days later encountered Admiral Blake, whose squadron had been anchored off Rye. Admiral Blake sailed up the channel as soon as news reached him that the Dutch were off Dover. There was a fairly brisk engagement but out of range of the Dover gunners. Admiral Maarten Tromp withdrew after losing two ships and sailed to Calais, whilst Admiral Blake anchored off the port.

It was not until 1716, however, that the Royal Regiment of Artillery came into being. The defence of Dover and other major strategic ports became the task of the Royal Garrison Artillery and numerous forts around the coast were built to house them. Later the Records Office of the Artillery was housed in Cliff Block—Dover Castle and later to become the Regimental Headquarters of 519 (K & S) Coast Regiment in the 1939/45 War. It was from Cliff Block that all the administration of the garrison regiments by way of postings, pay, promotions and sustenance, etc., was carried out.

During the Napoleonic wars, the Strait was patrolled constantly by the Channel Squadron to deny the French the full use of their Channel ports and to discourage Napoleon from any ideas of a mass invasion. The ships of the channel squadron, in all weathers, were always on station, and when some respite could be made, whilst the ships rearmed and revictualled, and anchored either in the Deal roads or off Dover, the men of Nelson would visit the inns and residences of the two old towns. There also existed a very lively trade in smuggling, especially between Deal and Kingsdown and the French ports. Customs cutters were constantly alert in the Channel to intercept this traffic, but the odds were always on the smugglers, who had their own early warning devices.

The Strait was very active during the Kaiser war. The port was commanded by Admiral Bacon and later by Sir Roger Keyes, R.N. Their headquarters were at Fleet House, a residence at about the centre of the seafront, before the erection of the present buildings. Admiral Sir Roger Keyes was most anxious to close the channel to all German shipping, especially the passage of submarines through the Straits on their way to the Atlantic sea lanes. Fortunately during the 1914/18 war, the French coast was friendly, and efforts were made to stretch a boom

across the Strait, supported by armed guard boats and trawlers. A gate operated by the Navy would be opened and shut to permit the passage of merchant shipping in convoy. The scheme was only partly successful. The guard vessels were repeatedly subject to attack by enemy destroyers. One such action took place on 21st April, 1917, when the Germans dispatched a number of destroyers and supporting craft to force the passage off Dover. They were met by the British destroyers, *H.M.S. Broke* and *H.M.S. Swift*, captained by Commanders Evans and Peck. The German flotilla was engaged and, after some very heavy fighting, two small German destroyers, *G.42* and *G.25* were sunk. The remainder then returned to their bases. The British suffered 57 casualties, 21 being killed, but 40 German survivors were picked out of the water and made prisoners of war. There is also mention of an enemy submarine surfacing in Langdon Bay, and firing a number of shells into the town. The Langdon guns could not be depressed sufficiently to engage and the Breakwater guns were masked by the Eastern Arm. She was not therefore engaged, and before the Navy could take action, had sailed away, no doubt well satisfied with her cheeky but nevertheless brave act.

There were frequent actions in the channel during the first world war, between destroyers and other light craft, but no concentrated attack on the port itself was ever made or indeed was the port threatened.

It was from Dover on St. George's Day, 1918 that *H.M.S. Vindictive* (Captain Carpenter) led 75 ships to an attack on the German held port of Zeebrugge, in an endeavour to seal the port and adjacent locks, so preventing German submarines using it as a base for their North Atlantic operations. Many gallant lives were lost that day and many decorations for the highest degree of gallantry were won. The attack was partially successful and the *Vindictive* was able to return home. A similar attempt

The royal salute for King Henry VIII on his embarkation from Dover in May 1520 for the Field of the Cloth of Gold.

on the port of Ostend, however, failed. It is perhaps ironic that the large bell rung by the Germans to give warning of the attack by the British, now hangs on the walls of the Dover Town Hall, and is by tradition, sounded on Zeebrugge Day.

The town and port was nearly destroyed by an instrument of its own making on 16th September, 1918. The monitor, *H.M.S. Glatton*, some 5700 tons, was anchored in the harbour and fully loaded with ammunition and explosives to carry to the army in France, when she caught fire. If she had exploded, the results could well have been catastrophic. The seafront houses were cleared and in fact a barrier put up in the Market Square to prevent onlookers getting any closer. After fighting the fire for some time, it became obvious that it would not be brought under control in time to prevent an explosion. Admiral Keyes, with reluctance, was forced to the inevitable decision of ordering a destroyer to torpedo *H.M.S. Glatton*. Being a monitor she was almost flat bottomed, but three torpedoes were fired into her at close range, so that she turned turtle almost immediately. Many men on board had little time or no time to escape, and so perished. She was not raised until 1925, when she was then towed to the Camber still upside down and plates were

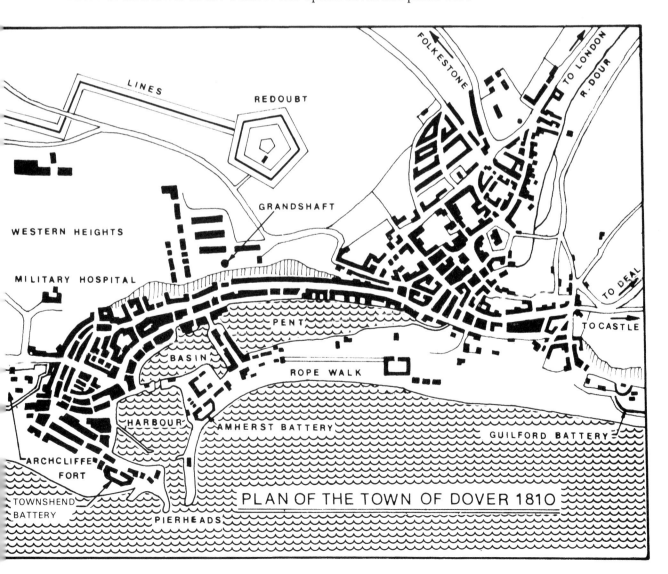

PLAN OF THE TOWN OF DOVER 1810

removed from her bottom, to allow the bodies to be removed, and the shells unloaded. A service was conducted on the upturned hull.

As in the second world war, the thought uppermost in the Defence Chief's mind was how to close the channel to enemy shipping. It was decided to construct enormous concrete towers — some in fact were assembled at the port of Richborough — and to equip these towers with searchlights and some armament. The towers would be spread across the channel, and by the liberal use of sea minefields, force a submarine to the surface, where it could then be engaged effectively. The idea was similar to the boom controlled by the trawlers, who were much more vulnerable to attack by a U-boat. The war however ended before they could be put to effective use, which was perhaps just as well, as they would have been very difficult to raise or destroy and would have remained a hazard in what are now the busiest shipping lanes in the world. It is interesting to note that one such tower still exists. It is called the Nab Tower, and stands in the sea approaches to the entrance of Spithead, a few miles off the Isle of Wight. During the last war it was armed with coast artillery defences as well as anti-aircraft guns. Today it is no more than a light beacon, well known to the yachtsmen and mariners alike.

The story of the defence of Dover in the second world war will be told in detail in a later chapter. What has been written above is only a very brief outline to illustrate the importance of the waters of the Dover Strait, some of the many and vicious actions they have witnessed, and the importance of the town and port itself, especially to an enemy.

H.M.S. Glatton in Dover Harbour after the explosion.

2 The weapons

Guns of all sizes and calibres have surrounded the old port since the cannon became a weapon of the British Army. Some old fortresses have disappeared altogether, whilst others still remain, overgrown by grass and weeds, derelict and forlorn in their great age, remembering past glories, when as spick and span new batteries, manned by keen volunteers in their pill box hats, they proudly pointed their muzzles across the Channel and defied any unwanted intruder to attempt to set his foot on English soil. They now only await final destruction from the hands of the bulldozer so that the very ground they now occupy can be used in one form of development or another to satisfy the ever increasing demand for space. Their role, like the cross-bowman of old, has gone, and defence is now placed in the hands of other instruments far more deadly and sinister. Even their more modern sisters, the great batteries of the last World War, lie forsaken and dejected, the prey of vandals. The

An Armstrong 110 pounder gun dated 1861, like those installed at Shoulder of Mutton Battery in Dover Castle.

guns themselves have long since been removed, but the few sites that remain are a scandal. They should at least be afforded a decent burial, and not left as hazards to young children, or objects to be defaced and defiled by those too young to know what service and sacrifice they have rendered their country but 40 years ago.

Many of the old gun emplacements still serve the community by providing enclosures in which wooden seats have been placed so that the visitor can rest himself and admire the sea view, quite unaware of the blood, toil and sweat of local volunteers of a bygone era who manned the defence works. Some old emplacements may be seen just above Archcliffe Fort on the road to the Channel Tunnel excavations, and others on the Admiralty Pier.

Some old forts have left no trace. The batteries of Amherst and Townshend, were sited each side of the entrance to the old tidal harbour, and close to where the Clock Tower now stands. They were armed with 4 x 32 pounders (Amherst) and 2 x 24 pounders (Townshend). It was always believed, and rightly so, that if the country were to be invaded, Dover would be the focal point and therefore must be made impregnable. Capture Dover and the road would be open to London.

The Amherst Battery.

In 1862, for reasons best known to those in authority, it was decided to turn Dover into a mighty fortress. At the time Britain was facing no severe threat from the continent. The French had recently been our allies in the Crimean war, but the old suspicions and jealousies remained, and France had a very formidable fleet.

The first fort to be built in 1862 was Fort Burgoyne. It was designed and built by Captain du Cane, R.E. The fort is sited on the eastern side of the town, on top of what is now known as Castle Hill and Connaught barracks. It was armed with no less than 29 guns in the ramparts and a further 6 guns in the casemates. 26 guns were sited in caponiers and flank batteries. East Wing Battery had a further 4 guns and West Wing Battery 5 guns. The total cost of this massive defence works was £88,053. This was indeed a very formidable fortress outside the castle complex, and obviously intended as defence works against an enemy landing well to the east of the town, possibly St. Margaret's Bay, Kingsdown or Deal as no other nearer landing ground presents itself, unless Langdon Hole was then considered a potential danger. Certainly no airborne attack could then have been envisaged. Strategically the fort protected the east flank of the town and castle and would have to be over-run by an enemy advancing from the east. During the last war, the fort was not armed or even came into the reckoning as a defence works.

The mad rush for the defence of Dover continued with the construction of the Shoulder of Mutton Battery within the Castle boundaries in 1862. The battery was armed with 2 x 110 pounder RBL

FORTIFICATIONS ON THE WESTERN HEIGHTS
DOVER C. 1945

15

Armstrong guns and was built to supplement the Castle defences. Its arc of fire was a splendid one, being sited on top of the cliff and fairly near the edge, also more or less covering the centre of the harbour as it is today. Of course in those days, before Dover Harbour was constructed, the waters in front of the Castle were merely anchoring grounds for vessels not wishing to enter the old tidal harbour. Unlike Fort Burgoyne, Shoulder of Mutton Battery was obviously intended as an anti-ship battery. It was not armed or used in any capacity in the last war and in fact no anti-ship battery was sited and armed within the castle defences during the two Great Wars. A battery for the purposes of firing royal salutes and other similar compliments did exist, just below the officers' mess, up to 1939 but since then this also has been discontinued. High personages seldom use the port as their arrival point, as they seem to prefer air travel. On the rare occasions when a dignitary is due to arrive at Dover, a battery has to be obtained, often as far away as Sussex or Hampshire to pay the appropriate compliment. The garrison regiments, usually three or four before the war, provided the guard of honour on the Marine Station.

The Defence Minister's eyes were now turned to the westward side of the port. Here there were many old defence works and deep moats dating back to the Napoleonic era, many in fact having been built with the assistance of French prisoners-of-war. A complicated system of wide moats and casemates, with gates and drawbridges, stretched like a maze across the Western Heights, and no doubt would have been a serious obstacle in the path of troops and cavalry of 18th and early 19th century. They offered no protection to the town and port itself, but obviously would have to be overcome if a potential enemy wished to establish a beach-head or base in Dover, before proceeding to London. Quite possibly those who were responsible for defence, regarded these vast earthworks as the outer London defences, but they would not have been difficult to contain and then by-pass by a determined enemy.

It was decided to supplement these earthworks with a chain of defences and batteries, with an anti-ship and anti-invasion role. The slope of the ground from the top of the Shakespeare cliff to the top of the hills beyond, lent itself to the construction of well sited batteries, the height giving additional range and well compensated any loss of range by dead ground in front of the battery. In 1867 and 1869 Drop Battery with 4 x 42 pounders and 1 x 7 inch RBL Armstrong gun, and Drop Redoubt with 17 guns on terreplein (15 in caponiers), were built. Drop Redoubt on the eastern end of the Western Heights, more or less overlooking the present day Maritime Hall could also cover the town. Drop battery came within the Citadel precincts. These two batteries cost the Exchequer some £35,577.

Near the top of the heights, and within the Citadel complex, North Centre Bastion battery was built in 1869 and armed with 15 guns on terreplein and 6 guns in flanking casemates. This battery cost £52,251, not an inconsiderable sum in those days, when no possible threat of invasion could be envisaged. It seemed that the policy to fortify an area in anticipation of invasion lapsed when that threat became a reality. All these batteries were obsolete before the outbreak of the first world war, and the sites were of little use. Perhaps they acted as a deterrent or to impress any foreigner landing in Dover, that the country was bristling with guns, and to accept their solemn warning.

However the construction of these defences continued unabated. Western Outworks, part of the Citadel complex was built in 1869 at a cost of £86,143. It contained 27 guns on terreplein and 14 guns in caponiers and casemates. It had accommodation for three officers and 181 other ranks. Large infantry barracks had been built on the cliffs behind Snargate Street called South Front Barracks and it is interesting to note that this section of the heights and barracks could be reached by a shaft, called Grand Shaft, containing spiral steps from ground level to the top of the cliff. A sentry was always mounted on guard at the entrance, for what purpose I do not know, for as a small boy I have often made my way up all these stone steps to the top of the cliff, and then across the top down into Folkestone Road. The shaft itself contained at least three sets of steps and clearly marked. 'Officers only', 'Warrant Officers and Senior N.C.O's' and 'Junior N.C.O's and Privates'. I never recall, however, anyone being checked for going up the wrong steps and all were in fact exactly the same. The officers' steps were not carpeted!

In 1862, the army estimates were £16,000,000 against the naval estimates of £11,000,000. Furthermore as an additional safeguard against invasion, a further sum of £2,000,000 for new fortifications and two years later a further £1,200,000 was allotted. These sums were expended on numerous forts mainly along the south coast from Pembroke to Sheerness and the Medway, Dover's allocation being £190,718. The navy on 1st January, 1863 consisted of 1,014 ships of all classes. Of this number there were 85 ships of line mounting from 74 to

South Front Barracks Western Heights.

The Channel Squadron in the 1860s.

131 guns each; 39 ships of from 50 guns to 72 guns each; 69 frigates of from 24 guns to 46 guns each; 30 screw corvettes each mounting 21 guns and upwards of 600 vessels of all classes mounting less than 20 guns. In addition there was a fleet of 190 gun-boats each mounting two heavy Armstrong guns. There were also numerous wooden mortar vessels, built during the Russian war and now laid up and rotting in Chatham. 43 new vessels were under construction and it was hoped to put them into service by the end of 1863. All these vessels then serving with the navy, were scattered all over the world. Some were on the Australian station and 32 vessels were on the East India and China station. Several vessels were employed on the west coast of Africa for the suppression of the slave trade and 29 vessels were still in North American waters. The Mediterranean squadron consisted of 28 vessels of all classes. The channel squadron consisted of but five ships, all iron plated, and the purpose of giving the reader these statistics, is to make the point that in the absence of any superior naval help in the event of attack or invasion, the country would have to rely on its own coast defences to repel an invader. There would certainly be no time for the not inconsiderable British fleet to be stationed in the channel.

In 1869, two further coast defence batteries were built. On the Western Heights, was South Front Battery, whose site has recently been levelled to make way for playing fields for the Borstal. The battery had 18 guns on terreplein and 12 in casemates, with accommodation for 14 officers and 436 other ranks. It cost no less than £54,520. The other battery, known as Castle Heights, was merely a casemated barrack for 72 men built under the east front ramparts of the castle at a cost of £6,683.

By 1872 it was decided to improve old ARCHCLIFFE FORT on the cliffs but at the foot of the western slopes; first a pit prepared for Moncrieff pattern 1 x 7 inch RBL as a practice battery and thirteen years later in 1885, 5 x 10 inch RML on Elswick platforms and one 7 inch RBL on Moncrieff pattern 1, disappearing carriage.

It now seemed that this wild orgy of spending on the Dover defences had come to an end. None of the guns was fired in anger and only a few used in practice. They were manned by troops of the Royal Garrison Artillery, but a majority of the man-power was provided by volunteers from the town.

There were two further extraordinary guns worthy of mention. These were two 81 tonners installed on the Pier Turret which was then the end of the Admiralty Pier, and now about halfway along the mole. They were called the Dover Turret and their mechanism is illustrated and fully explained in a book on coastal defences by the well known military historian Ian V. Hogg. It suffices to relate that they were capable of firing a shell weighing 1700 lbs from a gunpowder charge of 420 lbs. Work was actually commenced in 1880 but the battery was not fully operational until 1886. The purpose of this massive fortification was to ensure that guns able to pierce the thickest armour plating on ships were available to defend the port. They were sited in a turret some 33 feet above sea level and power was provided by a steam engine, actually below sea level. During the last war, whilst inspecting these great guns, I endeavoured to climb down by a narrow cat ladder to the gloom of the engine room. Little could be seen, except rust and corroded metal and about 18 inches of sea water on the floor. The giant barrels themselves were in excellent condition. At one time during the war years, the metal was considered as salvage scrap, but fortunately it was found that it would be too expensive to cut up and remove. There are reports that when they were installed, the garrison commander at the time was Lt.-General Lord Russell, and he ordered the total garrison, then 1000 men, to man the guide ropes, blocks and other equipment, to ensure the guns were properly put into, positioned and housed in the turret, a massive undertaking, even in those days. The cost of the equipment was said to be about £10,000, but the guns, like their sisters on the hills above them, were never fired in anger. Four proofing rounds were fired but in view of the reported damage to local property by way of broken windows and lost chimney pots they were never fired again and finally became obsolete in 1902. These great guns are still there today, but alas no longer accessible to the public. When I last saw them the barrels were in a depressed position. The chamber itself was colossal, well capable of absorbing any recoil. I felt sorry for the young lad whom I am told was expected to crawl up the barrels after firing to sponge out, but I have no doubt he was proud to do so.

Two further batteries with more modern equipment were built in 1900. First Citadel Battery containing 3 x 9.2 Mk 10 on mounting Barbette Mk 5. This is sited on the very top of the heights and overlooking Shakespeare cliff. It is now inside the Borstal compound. The other battery was Langdon. This battery was sited on the east side of the castle, overlooking Langdon Bay and east of the Eastern Arm mole. Originally it had two 10 inch BL guns but these were removed in 1912. By 1915 its armament consisted of three 9.2 guns and two 6 inch CP2. The 9.2 guns were removed in the 1920's and sent to the far east. These two batteries played their part during the last war and their story will be related later.

During the Kaiser war, it was decided to mount guns on the moles which made up the harbour. The old forts described above had become obsolete and their guns museum pieces. In 1915, the end of the Eastern Arm was equipped with two 12 pounder guns in an anti-motor torpedo boat role. South Breakwater Battery was built on the centre mole in 1915 and given two 6 inch guns Mk 7. Its only access was by boat and, contrary to general belief, there is no passageway under the sea either to the Admiralty Pier or Eastern Arm. Pier Turret Battery, situated about halfway down the Admiralty Pier and immediately above the old 81 tonners was equipped the same year also with two 6 inch Mk 7 guns and at the end of the same pier two 12 pounder guns in an anti-motor torpedo boat role, were installed. These then were the weapons available for the defence of the port at the beginning of the first world war and with only a change on the Eastern Arm, by the replacement of the twelve pounders for twin six pounders, the same weapons were available at the commencement of the second world war.

3 The men who manned them

So we pass on to the history of the local volunteers and territorials of the 20th century, leaving behind the old gunners who serviced the muzzle loaders on the hills each side of the town in the 18th and 19th centuries.

In 1907, the Territorial Army came into being. The Cinque Port Volunteers stood down, and in 1908, the 3rd Company Kent Garrison Artillery was formed. They enlisted for a 4 year engagement with an optional engagement at the end of that period, and a compulsory training period of not less than 45 drills per annum plus an annual camp of not less than 14 days. They trained in the Drill Halls provided in Liverpool Street, now demolished, which had both a large hall for drill instruction, and at the rear an even larger hall which was used as a riding school. They also used the older and smaller facilities, provided by Archcliffe Fort.

In 1914, Nos. 40 and 46 Companies Royal Garrison Artillery and one Company Kent R.G.A. (TF), manned the Citadel Battery, Pier Turret, Pier Extension, Eastern Arm, Southern Breakwater and Langdon Batteries. The total armament available for the defence of the port was 5 x 9.2 guns, 6 x 6 inch guns, and 5 x 12 pounder guns.

At the end of the Kaiser war, it was decided in 1920, to form the Kent Heavy Brigade with five batteries: 166 Heavy Battery at Rochester, 167

The Admiralty Pier Turret, the end of the original pier.

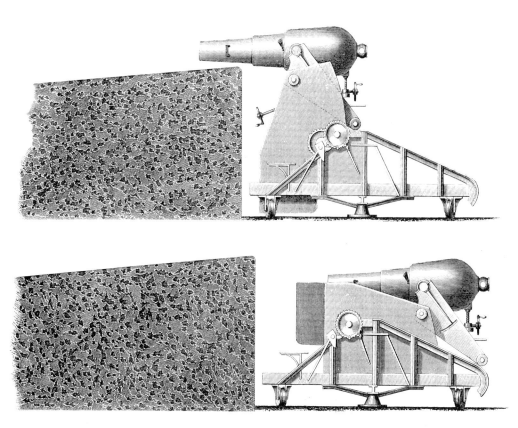

Heavy Battery at Gravesend, 168 Heavy Battery at Dover, 169 Heavy Battery at Sheerness, and 170 Heavy Battery at Ramsgate. A further battery, 159, covered Brighton and Lewes. The Coast Artillery School, the Mecca of coast gunners, where all courses and training in Coast Artillery were carried out, was Shoeburyness. In 1920 the men manning the coast guns were still regular soldiers of the R.G.A. supplemented by the Territorials. By the end of 1926, the War Office decided that the whole of the coast defence of the U.K. should be taken over by the Territorial Army, with one or two regular officers and warrant officers attached to each regiment for the purpose of training and administration. A regular regimental sergeant major as well as an adjutant were also attached to the regiments. The manning of the Coast Artillery searchlights became the responsibility of the Fortress Royal Engineers Territorial Army. The general organisation came directly under a Brigadier R.A. Coast Defences under the B.R.A.

In 1932, yet another reorganisation took place, when the Kent and Sussex Batteries were merged into one regiment, the Kent and Sussex Heavy Brigade R.A.T.A. with its Regimental Headquarters at the Liverpool Street Drill Hall, Dover, and three Batteries, 168 at Dover, 170 at Ramsgate and 159 at Brighton, each recruiting from the surrounding towns and districts. For example, a number of men were recruited from Folkestone for the Dover Battery, and Ramsgate covered Margate and the nearby towns. Brighton included the town of Lewes. In the event of an emergency, the Brigade would man the Dover defences and those of Newhaven.

In 1939 'brigade' was removed from the title and the regiment was renamed Kent and Sussex Heavy Regiment R.A.T.A., but in 1940 it changed its name yet again to 519 (K & S) Coast Regiment R.A. However by then its responsibilities had been divided by the formation of a second regiment, 520 Coast Rgt. R.A. It was decided that '519' should retain the batteries surrounding the harbour, namely Pier Turret, Pier Extension, South Breakwater, Eastern Arm and the examination Battery Langdon. The Fire Command Post would remain on top of the cliffs, in front of Cliff Block and directly beneath the Naval Port War Signal Station. (It is still there today.) '520' would take over the Citadel Battery and later Lydden Spout, Hougham and Capel. '519' would later acquire an emergency battery, Western Heights, sited in the location of the old St. Martin's Battery area. Yet a third regiment was formed in 1941 to control the newly erected long range batteries at Fan Bay, Wanstone, and South Foreland. Both 520 and 540 were given their own Fire Command Posts, but tactically were controlled by the Coast Artillery Operations Room in Dover Castle. A further off-shoot of 519 came into being in 1940 by the formation of the 5th Super Heavy Regiment. This was a railway mounted battery, sited near Shepherdswell tunnel, and equipped with 12 inch guns.

It is well worth dwelling a little on the history of the Dover battery up to the outbreak of the second war. They had acquitted themselves well and were known throughout the Coast Artillery world. They won the King's Cup in the Territorial Army Competitions 1927 and again in 1933.

Opposite
The Moncrieff gun such as was installed at Archcliffe Fort in 1885 gave protection for the gun crew by being installed in a pit.

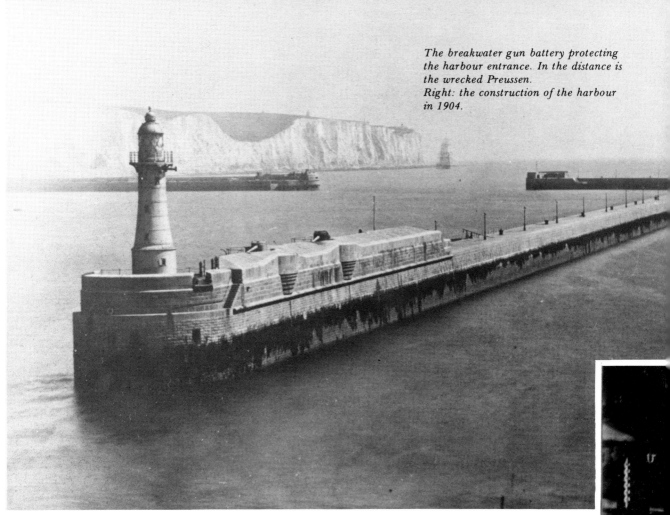

They could well have won another in 1938 but having reached the last three batteries in the U.K. a cartridge was inserted the wrong way round, causing a misfire and valuable loss of time. The King's Cup was competed for each year by the 9.2 batteries of the U.K. and the efficiency, drill and accuracy of fire was judged by regular army instructor gunners and assistant instructor gunners from the School of Gunnery. The competition was an extremely keen and hard fought contest, bringing considerable pride and prestige to the winner. The handsome King's Cup was retained by the winners for all time.

168 Battery continued its success by being second in the City of London Cup in 1930, second in the King's Cup in 1926, and were then awarded the Prince of Wales Cup. They reached the final again at Penlee in 1939, but were mobilised before the competition could be completed. They also won numerous other trophies for boxing in the Territorial competitions, and also for rifle shooting. A rifle competition was held each year, and competed by all the local Territorial units of all services, and confined to Dover. These included not only the anti-aircraft and coast gunners, but also the Royal Engineers from Archcliffe Fort and a battalion of Buffs from the old sea-plane shed they used for a

Drill Hall on the Dover seafront. The infantry were almost duty bound to win the trophy, known as the Emden Trophy, after a former mayor of Dover, but considerable rivalry existed between the units, and 168 Battery had their fair share of wins. The competition always took place on the Lydden Spout rifle ranges, at various ranges up to 500 yards.

As will now become obvious, all efforts were directed by the local battery on their favourite equipment, the 9.2 guns at Citadel. A concentration of training of layers, rangefinders, battery commander's assistants, gun loaders, gun position officers, etc., etc., became intensified, with one goal in mind — the winning of the King's Cup and to be classified as the straightest shots with a 9.2 in the country. The unit's bible was a small blue book, called Coast Artillery Training Vol. 1, with numerous amendments, which had to be carefully pasted in. Every officer had a copy of this book, as did the warrant officers, and senior N.C.O.'s and everybody tried to assimilate its complicated gunnery contents and calculations, and to understand its army jargon, bearing in mind that, after all, we were very ordinary civilians who only wore a uniform at weekends.

4 Getting ready

But ye say 'It will mar your comfort' ye say 'It will minish our trade'.
Do ye wait for the spattered shrapnel, ere ye learn how a gun is laid?
For the low, red glare to southward when the raided coast towns burn?
(Light ye shall have that lesson, but little time to learn.)

Kipling, *The Islanders*, 1902.

On joining the Territorial Army on 1st May, 1937 as a second lieutenant, I was required to attend the Liverpool Street Drill Hall every Tuesday and Thursday, and most weekends. If practice seawards was to be carried out, that is the actual firing of the guns at a moving sea target, my presence was essential for at least eight hours. If I attended eight hours, I was awarded pay and sustenance allowance amounting to 50p in total. With the exception of annual camp, no other monetary award was forthcoming.

I was further required to provide myself with two service dress jackets, riding breeches, properly cut and complying with army regulations, field boots and spurs, a Sam Browne, frog and sword, great coat and head gear for both service and mess occasions. Furthermore at least three khaki shirts and tie, patrol jacket and patrol trousers with dress spurs, and an artillery mess jacket with all the appropriate badges of rank. I had also to provide myself with a camp bed, canvas bath and bucket, canvas wash basin on a stand and a large canvas roll-up valise with broad leather straps to carry the whole lot and one's other gear. This completed the required and necessary accoutrements of a young Territorial officer.

The government in a small way, partly compensated one by making a grant toward the cost, after purchase, providing the Commanding Officer was satisfied that everything had been acquired and fitted, of about £30. This sum in no way covered the expenditure which was nearer £100, but it helped.

I was somewhat embarrassed as well as self-conscious when I reported on the first day in uniform. It was 8.30 on a Sunday morning and the battery was going up to the Citadel for training on the guns. I was met at the entrance to the Drill Hall by a battery sergeant major, a regular soldier, who was also the permanent staff instructor, as well as being the local recruiting officer, which was all part of his duties. He informed me, very politely, indeed he proved to be a very kindly man, that whilst I had assembled myself fairly well, and looked in good shape, the adjutant to whom I was required to report, would not be at all pleased to see the Sam Browne cross strap across my left shoulder instead of my right. It brought home to me that I was very much a Civilian in uniform.

The establishment of personnel before the war were all posted from regular army units and attached to the T.A. for training and administration. They consisted of the adjutant, R.S.M., the P.S.I. holding W.O. 2 rank, and one or two civilian clerks. Each battery had its own P.S.I. The commanding officer was a Territorial, holding the rank of Lt. Colonel, but he lived in Brighton, so we did not see him very often, except on inspections and practice seawards. He retired in 1939 and our own battery commander was promoted to command the regiment.

There was usually a good attendance at the weekday parades, although two of our officers lived in and near London, and only came down at weekends. There was always a full attendance on Sundays, or the adjutant would want to know the reason why. We had to have a very good reason indeed for non-attendance. The Dover battery, before the war, consisted of a major, as battery commander, two battery captains, and four subalterns. The B.C. was a chartered accountant in London, the battery captains a solicitor in Bromley and an architect in London, whilst the subalterns were a chartered accountant, an insurance official and two bank clerks. In addition the battery ran a ladies' guild which organised social outings, dances and the children's Christmas party. As I lived on the Dover seafront and nearest to the Drill Hall, they usually used to meet in my house under the chairmanship of my wife, but in fact it was the battery sergeant major's wife, a very large and somewhat forbidding woman, who usually took charge. She was very competent, and under her guidance and advice to my wife, the Ladies' Social Guild functioned very well.

The battery consisted of about 100 men from all walks of life, and nearly all resident in Dover. A few came from Folkestone. The Post Office, East Kent Road Car Company, Co-operative Stores, and Wiggins Teape Paper Mill provided the bulk of our battery but we also had a few miners, bank clerks, insurance clerks, corporation officials and quite a variety of other trades and professions. We also had a local doctor, but he only used to attend camp. His wife was also a doctor and looked after his practice whilst he was away. We were, all in all, quite a happy little family. The adjutant looked upon the subalterns as the biggest and most incompetent creatures it had been his misfortune to encounter during all his military service and he was probably quite right. If he was not there to watch over us, the regimental sergeant major was, and we were almost as frightened of him as we were of the adjutant, knowing full well that any misdemeanour on our part, would draw condemnation from him and if we did not take him seriously, he would certainly report us to the adjutant. We called our adjutant 'teeth and tonsils' possibly due to his loud voice and insistence that every so often he made us carry out shouting drill, to strengthen our voices. Although we did not realise it at the time, these two regular soldiers were quite dedicated men. They certainly had the knowledge and were doing their best to mould a bunch of happy-go-lucky civilians, who regarded playing at soldiers as being a hobby, into an efficient team. War clouds, although still distant, were nevertheless rising, and they realised that they had a job to do and they did it to the best of their ability. I met the adjutant again at the latter end of the war and shortly before he died of a disease contracted in the east. I was then a major, and was able to express to him my grateful thanks for the background and basic training he had given me, although I had not appreciated it at the time.

The weekday training from 7 p.m. to 9 p.m. was divided into a number of small groups, such as gun layers classes, rangetakers, dummy loaders, map reading and miniature range. This latter piece of ingenious equipment consisted of a board, supported horizontally at each corner by four posts about six feet high. The board contained numerous holes about two or three inches apart. There was a dark background, with black curtains across the front. In the centre of the board, a small model ship was fixed to a pivot, with a dial beneath, marked in degrees. When training took place on this piece of equipment, the wretched subaltern would take up his position at the other end of the drill hill on a kind of raised desk. The curtain on the range was pulled to one side, and peering through the binoculars, the subaltern would focus on the small model ship. He would note the approximate direction and angle she appeared to be going. The instructor would then give him the order to engage, and he would then issue all the necessary orders prior to firing. 'Alarm, Case 11, take post, target destroyer moving right, 130 degrees, add 100, Fire.' A gentleman standing beneath the board on the miniature range, having allowed a suitable interval for time of flight, would push two sticks through the holes in the board, to represent the shell splashes. If this operator had had a bad day at his office or work, you could be sure the splashes were a long way from the target and to make it more difficult, some distance apart. The subaltern, by a series of corrections, shouted loud enough for the operator to hear, would be required to bring the splashes together and in line with the target. He would then commence the Rules of Ranging, which he was supposed to know, usually 'Ladder Fire', until he crossed the target, the range operator applying his corrections to the splashes, the holes reckoned to be 50 yards apart. The battery commander's assistant would carefully take down all orders and observations made by the B.C. on a prepared recording form, and at the end of the shoot, always providing it got that far without being stopped by the confused and bewildered B.C., the P.S.I. or adjutant would explain, very forcibly, everything that had gone wrong and the reasons why it had gone wrong. In fact, there seldom seemed to be anything right. Anyway I practised away, not without a little concern and worry, as well as private tuition from the adjutant and the P.S.I. outside drill hours. On reflection it seemed that they were quite happy to give up their spare time, just to coach the uninitiated. In point of fact, when the conflict did come, I never once used all this complicated ranging and laddering, as the whole system shortly after the commencement of hostilities was abandoned. But at least we all tried and tried very hard. Even whilst at work during the day, I found myself, repeating again and

again, the opening orders for fire, and my well thumbed Coast Artillery Vol. 1 was a constant companion. It did not seem at all strange to me, during my lunch hour, when I used a small cafe in Dover, to have C.A.T. Vol. 1 propped up against a glass whilst I consumed my meal.

The book contained the whole set up of a fortress system of range finding, calculations, manning parades, etc. There were details of the organisation of a coast fortress in peacetime, and in war, fighting a counter-bombardment action, fighting a close defence action, rangefinders, vertical base and depression finders, the short horizontal base and correction gears. All deep mysteries to me. The book revealed other mysteries such as ballistics, laying, gunnery calculations and trigonometrical functions (not my strong point), apex angles, and barometric corrections, tide levels and effective limits of auto-sights with

The well-thumbed training manual— "an awful lot of useless knowledge."

datum and correction slide rules. Battery drill and fire discipline were not neglected; ranging and observation of fire were all fully explained. The book even went as far as setting out instructions for the training and examination in laying, and instructions for the examination for skill-at-arms badges for gunnery. If a gunner was successful in convincing a Board that he had mastered some of these crafts, he was entitled to wear the appropriate badge on his sleeve. Looking at my C.A.T. Vol. 1 today, it seems that we assimilated an awful lot of useless knowledge, suitable for the 1914/18 war, and a little to meet the war which was about to come.

Then there were the weekends, usually Sundays, (on Saturday we played rugby) when we would travel up to the great Citadel Battery of 2 x 9.2 guns, located where the Borstal Institution is today, and no doubt far more comfortable today than it was in 1937/39. It was not often that the sand filled 9.2 shells were available. They weighed 380 lbs and some wear was caused to the barrels, thus restricting their use. Also of course, a question of economy had to be considered, even in those days. However a 6 pounder gun with special attachment was fixed above the mounting, and whilst all the necessary 9.2 drill could be carried out and a moving target engaged, it was only the 6 pounder which fired, and the B.C. consequently had a much smaller splash to observe, although the range was shorter. The 6 pounder had a very sharp crack, so if one were appointed to the duty of safety officer, one was required to position oneself at the auto sight telescope, which was almost in direct line with the muzzle of the 6 pounder just above. The result was inevitably deafness and a nasty headache, but it was considered *infra dig* to use cotton wool. I was told to stand on my toes and open my mouth, and this would help to absorb the shock waves. The safety officer's job, by the way, was merely to ensure that the gun was more or less pointing in the right direction, and not laid on a ship or the wretched target vessel. If it was, there was not a lot the safety officer could do, but yell 'Stop' at the top of his voice. On occasions we also manned the anti M.T.B. guns, 12 pounders, on the Pier Extension, and they had a one inch rifle tube inserted in their muzzles, as a means of economy. We even boasted of a 12 pounder gun in our drill hall, for training purposes which fired lead slugs at a small target. The 12 pounder was a grand gun. The layer was so wedged in that he traversed the gun with his body, whilst sighting the gun on target through his telescope. With his right hand he pulled the trigger, every time the loader shouted 'Ready'. In practice he invariably kept the trigger pressed, so that the gun fired as soon as the breech was closed. If there was not a nimble loader, he would hear a lot of bad language, as the recoil knocked the loader's knuckles.

The 6 inch on the Pier Turret and at Langdon were usually fired by the batteries who travelled up from Brighton (159) and from Ramsgate (170). We were taught three methods for firing the 6 inch and 9.2 inch. Auto-sight, which would be applied if the target were only at very short range or what was termed within the 'effective limit of auto-sight'. By this method the rangetakers both for bearing and range, laid the gun by applying their pointers in the telescopes on the bow water line of the target. If the tide levers had been applied correctly and the gun datumed with accuracy, the barrel would automatically be set at the exact quadrant elevation for the shell to hit the bow water line. It was up to the B.C. to apply the necessary corrections for wind, travel, and of course the part of the target he wished to hit. The second, and by far the most usual method we employed was CASE II. By this method, the gun was laid for line, visually, through the auto-sight telescope, but the range was transmitted by dials, from a rangefinder on a flank. At the Citadel we used a Depression Position Finder. This instrument tracks the target, by means of a powerful telescope, on a gridded chart, measures bearings and ranges from the gun for which it is set up to the target, and automatically transmits these bearings and ranges to electrical receiving dials, then called Watkins Dials and later a more modern version after the outbreak of war, known as Magslip Dials. The D.P.F. was an accurate instrument, depending on his height above sea level, the higher the better, and of course conditions of good visibility. The theory with this instrument and also the other vertical base instrument, the Depression Rangefinder, was as follows. The known height of the instrument is the base, the right angle between a vertical line through the instrument and the surface of the sea is one known angle of the

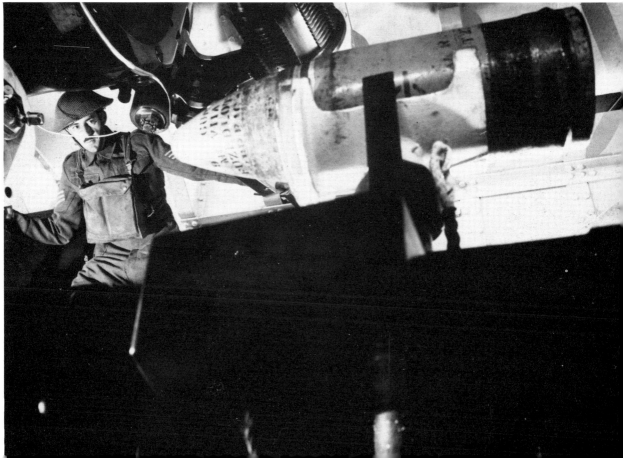

rangefinding triangle, and the other known angle is the angle of depression between a horizontal line through the instrument and the line of sight to the waterline of the target. The angle of depression varied with the range and is therefore a measure of the range to the target. This then is the method we used at the Citadel, and a similar, but smaller instrument, known as the Depression Rangefinder, whose range was limited to 12,000 yards, was used at Langdon and South Breakwater. Pier Turret's method was the use of a naval instrument, the Barr and Stroud.

The third and final method of fire was CASE III. By this means both range and line was transmitted by the rangefinder, and no visual means for laying on the gun itself, was employed. It will therefore be seen that to engage a target, it was essential for somebody actually to see it, be it the rangetakers on their vertical instruments or the layers through their telescopes on the gun. Radar was then unheard of, when targets could be engaged at long ranges and be entirely invisible.

There were two methods of fire open to us — (a) gun fire, when the guns were fired independently of each other at an interval ordered; and (b) salvo fire when the guns were fired simultaneously on the order or signal of a Gun Position Officer, and it is here that our voice training by the adjutant became invaluable. The only instrument available to use was a tin megaphone, no such refinements as microphones being available. The G.P.O. received his orders from the B.C., who telephoned them down to the G.P.O's assistant, and it was up to the G.P.O. to see that both guns were ready to fire when the order came. The No.1 of each gun indicated to the G.P.O. that he was ready, by raising his right hand, and woe betide the G.P.O. if both guns did not fire together.

As far as the battery commander himself was concerned his mind was occupied by the three methods of ranging open to him — viz:

Ranging by battery salvoes;
Ranging by ladder;
Ranging by one or more rounds of battery fire.

We had already had instruction on this somewhat complicated ladder fire and whilst the other two were easier, and self explanatory, it was by ladder we were invariably instructed to fire.

And so we made our way to the Citadel with these thoughts in mind. The officers used their own cars and the men were transported by truck. When we had gathered ourselves behind the guns and neatly stacked our rations of a meat pie and apple, supplied by our loving parents or wives, the battery commander would shout 'Manning Parade'. The two gun detachments would fall in, together with the rangetakers, telephonists, recorders and all the other sundry personnel in accordance with the drill laid down in our manual C.A.T. Vol. 1. The first job of the Section Commander was to check if enough people had turned up to carry out the shoot, and whether he had sufficient number of specialists. For instance, our key man on the D.P.F. happened to work in the G.P.O. If for any reason he happened to be on duty that particular Sunday, it meant a bit of changing round, but we managed in the end and I never

Opposite
9·2 inch Coastal Defence guns similar to those at the Citadel Battery showing the shell rack below the gun floor and a shell being lifted to the breach. (Imperial War Museum).

33

recall any shoot being held up through lack of specialists or personnel, although of course things went a lot smoother if you had the right men for the right jobs.

We were then instructed to draw stores and 'prepare for action'. The detachments were to repair to their respective guns, the B.C.'s staff to the B.O.P. the rangetakers to the cell about 400 yards to the flank to datum their D.P.F. and the G.P.O. with his signal staff and telephonists would climb on to a mound between the two guns on which stood a small tin shed. From here he would connect the telephone with the B.C. and ensure that first he had established communications. He also managed to set up a line to the D.P.F. cell. The Nos. 1 on each gun would set about preparing the equipment, checking the leads, examining obturation pads, datuming the autosight, and a dozen other jobs which took approximately one hour.

The subaltern upon whose shoulders had fallen the duties of Gun Position Officer, having satisfied himself that he had good communication on the ancient old telephone sets, which required winding with a handle to call up the recipient, would draw his tin megaphone, and prepare himself for the ghastly duty of pre-testing dials. In those days we used the old Watkins Dial. This was a system whereby the rangetakers on the position finder, set their dial to certain data ranges or test points, as they were then called. The ranges, having been set on the dial are passed electrically to a similar dial on each gun. It is obvious that the purpose of the test points were to ensure that the D.P.F. dials corresponded exactly to those on each gun on at least the test points as well as maximum range. If there was one thing certain in this life it was the fact that never, repeat never, did all three agree at the initial test point. It was probable that all three differed, and each gun when asked to report the reading on its dial would quote a range quite different from the range on the D.P.F. It was the job of the G.P.O. to get them all the same, and he could only do so by disconnecting one dial and running the others to the range on the disconnected dial. Then by connecting up again, he could be sure that at this stage at least two dials agreed, until he went to the second test point, when by some strange means, they all differed again, and the whole process had to be repeated. When they were finally put right, the G.P.O. had lost his voice completely. If he received the dreadful cry from the guns, 'Dial clicking but not working', it meant sending for an artificer and further delay in time. The dial checking was indeed a very frustrating job for the G.P.O. and he was lucky if he got them all working correctly and corresponding, in under an hour.

When the Nos. 1 of each gun reported, the G.P.O's next job would be to inspect them. He would ensure that the preparation for action had been carried out correctly and thoroughly and that everybody knew his job. The B.C. was very strict that no talking whatsoever, with the exception of No. 1, took place by any member of the detachment, except when called upon to report. There was a certain rivalry between Nos. 1 and 2 guns, which if anything, increased the efficiency of the detachments, and generally there was little to complain about the

keenness and enthusiasm of the men. The sergeants in charge of the gun were older men and in most cases certainly knew a lot more than the young subaltern, whose duty it was to inspect their equipment. On a number of occasions I received valuable help and advice, as well as knowledge from a gun No. 1 or an autosight layer, or even a leading number, for which I was very grateful. It was rather a queer set-up. A number of the men were in civilian life in the same job as myself and were probably senior to me, but that was how the pre-war Territorial Army worked. The final job of the inspecting G.P.O. was to fire an electrical tube to ensure that the electrical circuit on the gun was functioning, and should it break down, he also tested a percussion tube, should it become necessary to change the means of fire to percussion. There was one very dreadful occasion, when through ignorance, I had the gun traversed through 360 degrees, before the No. 1 could intervene. This had the effect of dragging all the electrical wires out of the dials, as they were not fitted with slip rings, and it took an artificer half the morning to repair the damage. When all was ready, the G.P.O. reported to the B.C. through his hand telephone, 'Battery ready for action'.

Major Frank Martin in front of a 6 inch gun at Langdon Battery.
Two views of the remains of the Citadel Battery. At the outbreak of war in 1939 the Battery, comprised of 9·2 inch Mark X guns on short-range mountings (17,000 yards).

There was of course in the meantime, a lot of paper work and calculations to be done by the officer who was to conduct the shoot, often, but not always, the B.C. himself. Sometimes he would detail one of the subalterns to carry out the shoot, to give him experience. There was a number of tests and calculations for the B.C. so that every avenue had to be explored to find the exact correction to apply to the guns to enable him to get a hit with the first salvo. There was the B.C.'s correction form which was compiled from information obtained from a table with data for calculating initial correction, the datum slide rule, particular to each battery, which allowed for trunnion height above sea level, muzzle velocity, the type of projectile, wear of barrel, charge temperature, jump, droop, corrected barometer and finally the BAR telegram, usually obtained from the local R.A.F. station, giving not only the present barometer reading, but also speed and direction of the wind at various heights. Having carried out all these complicated calculations on the B.C.'s correction form, the end result usually came out in 'clicks' to be applied to the autosight, for line or in yards, plus or minus, to be applied for range. Almost the same result could be found by wetting one's finger and holding it up to the wind. The left or right deflection according to the direction of the target, was nearly always the same and if you added 100 yards as an addition to the range for good measure, you were never very far out. To suggest such a thing in practice, however, would have been regarded as sacrilege. If the adjutant had ever learned of such a thing, it would have been extra duties and goodness knows what tortures he could think up.

At long last all would be ready and the B.C. would report to the Director of Practice, usually the colonel, that the battery was ready to commence firing. It was usually the sign for the channel to fill with traffic. It had been quite void of boats up till now. It invariably followed that once we were ready, and the old launch could start letting out her targets, small yachts would leave Dover harbour, to sail slowly over our range or get themselves becalmed, and vessels of all sorts, sizes, and descriptions, would appear, sailing up and down the Strait, as if they had by some magic means, been waiting over the horizon for us to get ready. And so the launch would sit happily at the appointed rendezvous, whilst the battery would sit down on the grass near the guns, until such time as the range cleared and we could jump into action. We have sometimes waited from 10.30 a.m. until 5 p.m. without firing a shot, and it certainly became tiring and frustrating. Of course there were other diversions in the form of courting couples on the grass, a long way away, on Shakespeare Cliffe. Little did they suspect that high powered telescopes and rangefinders from the large guns away on top of the ridge, were focused on them, and their every amorous activity observed. We were indeed Peeping Toms, but what else was there to do?

Perhaps a more pleasant and certainly less energetic task was the appointment to the duty of range officer. Together with a signaller and a recorder, a primitive form of radio, some sandwiches and a bottle of beer, one would be required to report to the Camber and board an ancient tug-like vessel, equipped for target-towing and named *Sir Robert*

*Whigham**; although she was affectionately known by many other less complimentary names. This vessel was capable of about 8 knots, and with a two knot tide with her could reach a speed of about 10 knots, towing behind her two lattice-work target floats, called, I know not why, Hong Kong floats. But alas, if the tide was running against her, her speed would be reduced considerably. Armed with a chart on which were inscribed a number of marked courses and rendezvous, all at various ranges, the old craft would puff her way to a pre-selected point and report 'Launch at rendezvous 1/2/3', as the case may be, to the Director of Practice. There she would sit, possibly all day, if there was a lot of shipping about in the Channel, especially small yachts if it was a good day for a sail. Safety regulations demanded at least five degrees clearance of any ship and to allow for richochets, at least a range and a half before the battery could open fire. The range officer acquainted himself with an instrument, set up in the stern, called a rake. This he would line up with the targets, by applying his eye to an eye-piece, and setting his rake-like instrument parallel with the line of fire. By doing so, he could observe the shell splashes or fall of shot and measure their distance either plus or minus of the floats. He could not tell if they were in line. The target floats were let out on a winch, some 800 yards astern and the means of measurement as calculated by prongs on the rake, representing 25 yard intervals. He would call out the plus or minus distances to the recorder and at the end of the shoot, the signaller would send the results back to the battery. The whole system was somewhat primitive, as the old vessel rolled about, and if the range officer was feeling at all seasick or the waves obstructed his view, he had some difficulty in sending back accurate results. Nevertheless, something had to be sent back and this he did. Too many unobserved reports would result in a wasted shoot and bring the wrath of the B.C. down upon his shoulders.

Before all this could take place, the target ship had to be instructed 'proceed on course'. She would pay out the cable with the Hong Kong floats, and when the required safety distance had been let out, she would charge down the course, belching smoke, and doing all of 8 knots. To increase the speed of the targets, she would winch them in, so the battery had a moving target of a least 12 knots. The battery perceiving she was ready to commence her run, and the channel being free of shipping, would send out the magic word 'Pip', and hoist a red flag. When 'engage' was given by the Director of Practice, firing commenced. There was always a great and familiar cry, 'red flag up in battery, wind up on launch'.

At the end of the practice, all the orders, recordings, range reports, etc. together with times and other complicated sets of figures, were written up on a large blackboard, ruled out for this purpose. We all gathered round, and the assistant instructor gunner, or the instructor gunner himself, would tell us the error of our ways. He would tell us that we should have added 200 yards at a certain stage, when we had only added 100 yards. We were therefore guilty of creeping. The times and ranges set on the dials were noted and the gun drill itself was criticised. I suppose we were expected to memorise the blackboard figures, for in our

* General Sir Robert Whigham was Deputy Chief of Imperial General Staff. 1916-18 and a former Commissioner of the Duke of York's R.M. School.

37

spare time we were expected to complete a large form, called a Practice Seawards Report, which required every possible detail on each sheet, with diagrams and explanations galore. I never did discover what actually happened to these practice reports, or where they finally came to rest, even if anyone ever bothered to read them. The adjutant demanded them within a week of the shoot, and that was the last time they were ever seen. Fortunately we were able to overcome some of our difficulties. One subaltern was a keen photographer, and would photograph the blackboard, so that we could retain the information thereon, before it was all rubbed out.

And so the training went on, week after week, more or less on the same lines, but the system worked. New recruits joined the battery, but it was not long before they were all sorted out, and took their place, according to their aptitude, in layers, rangetakers, or specialists classes. The more brawny ones usually finished up as loading numbers on the gun. We read the newspapers and stories about Hitler and dark clouds gathering over Europe. We read with sympathy the news about Czechoslovakia and Austria, much in the same way as one reads about crises in today's newspapers. It did not mean very much, and was soon forgotten in the everyday bustle of work and play. I am certain that it never occurred to us that we were being prepared and trained to meet those dark clouds, or that we would shortly stand by those Citadel 9.2 guns, with H.E. shells on our hoists instead of the usual sand-filled ones, and that it would not be too long before those guns, and one or two others, would be all that was standing between that man Hitler and the occupation of our country. The thought would have been quite unbelievable. It could happen to others, but never to us.

Another aspect of our training and preparation for war was the annual fifteen days camp, usually held at the end of July. We were all required to attend, under a dire penalty if we failed to do so. If a man failed to report for camp, without a highly satisfactory explanation beforehand, the local police could be sent round to his residence to collect. I do not recall such stringent measures ever being adopted in the Kent & Sussex Brigade. After all, everyone was a volunteer, and there would be no point in not turning up. Regrettably, it was overlooked that July was the height of the summer season and the time when the buses would require all their staff, the shops would be busy with the summer trade, and those of us in offices would have to go humbly to our bosses and ask for leave, at a time usually selected by our seniors for their holidays. We were not at all popular, and I was frequently told that if I wanted to go and play soldiers, I should go in November, when I would cause the least amount of inconvenience. I am certain this was quite common amongst the Territorials, but again this was the way Britain trained its civilian army and confronted it with every difficulty and trial, and it was looked upon as something rather amusing by those who were not its members. We should have been doing something more useful, like fishing or playing cricket, instead of dressing up and wasting our time pretending to be soldiers. All this, whilst foreign armies trained and trained, in their masses, and the Hitler youth movement, the Brown

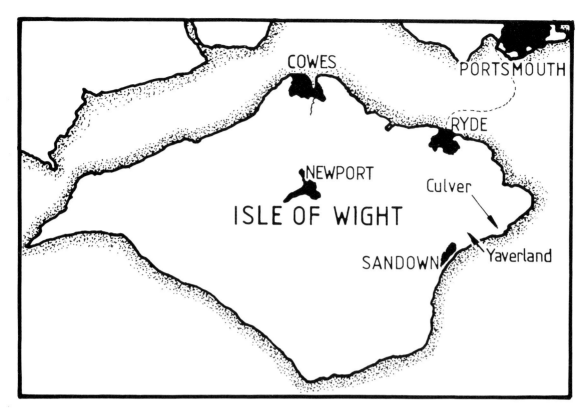

Shirts and all the other coloured shirts, with the full encouragement of their countries, prepared for the obvious conflict to come.

For camp, we usually went off to Yaverland Camp, on the Isle of Wight. It provided us with 12 pounder practice, and 6 inch and 9.2 practice at Culver, close by. The camp was a large tented one, with marquees for the various messes and battery offices. All of the latter proudly flew their battery flags and vied with one another, in battery and regimental crests, and presentations. All the regimental silver and cups were displayed in the officers', and sergeants' messes, and a great and professional air of military importance prevailed. The subalterns had one batman between two, and the more senior ranks a batman each. These were all men who had volunteered for the job. They were not expert gun layers or rangetakers, and were usually excused guard and fire picket, whilst so employed. The officers concerned themselves paid their batmen a princely sum of 50p per week, which in those days was quite a lot, and the senior officers always gave more than the minimum pay laid down. The officer/batman relationship was an excellent one; in fact the batmen vied with one another to see who could turn out the smartest officer. We now produced our canvas washstands and baths and buckets. Each morning we bravely washed outside our tents, in cold water, and I am quite sure we resembled the soldiers of the Boer war period, as customs could not have changed very much.

Each morning we went off for training on the guns, and to read the daily battery orders, to see who had been detailed as the next orderly

Territorial Army camp was held on the Isle of Wight at Yaverland.

officer, the next orderly sergeant, who was taking tomorrow's shoot and who was on the launch. Then there was afternoon drill, usually lectures or shouting drill for subalterns, and a new type of training was creeping into our curriculum. It was something nobody seemed to know much about and was known as P.A.D., or Passive Air Defence. We had a couple of Lewis guns, for drill purposes only, and had learned all the stoppages and merits and defects of this ancient weapon. Now people were talking about gas attacks, and detection, and air raid protection. It all seemed rather absurd to us. We could not protect ourselves or sit in shelters, if we had to man our guns, or whoever thought of laying a gun in a gas mask? But pamphlets and booklets appeared and it now formed part of our everyday training.

Except for about two night shoots and one guest night each week, when all the officers would be present, our other nights were free to spend in the hostelries of Sandown. On mess nights we were required to dress up in our mess jackets and spurs and eat a solemn meal. The junior subaltern, nominated as vice-president, would be called upon by the mess president, at the end of the meal to propose the loyal toast. This wretched subaltern was not allowed to leave the table until the colonel had retired, and if the colonel had a guest, he could go on chatting away to him for an hour after all the others had retired to the ante-room. Mr. Vice would be left, seated at the end of the table entirely on his own. But this was tradition and custom. This was how it had always been, and always would be and was readily accepted. Later, however, things livened up considerably. As soon as the C.O. had retired to his tent, mess games would commence. These were violent, rough and often dangerous. The new subalterns were required to make their exit through the ventilation flap in the marquee roof, with prodding forks in their bottoms, make their way across the marquee roof, and re-enter by way of the ventilation flap on the other side. Then, of course, there was always the traditional rugger match, usually with somebody's hat as the ball, causing destruction of the mess furniture, and inevitably, the tearing of one's overalls, and the staining of one's shirt, with beer. We did remove our jackets before play commenced. There was another violent game, known as high cock-alorum. Two officers lay on their backs on the floor, linking arms, with one leg in the air, endeavouring to link their legs, and turn each other over. If you were caught, and did not give way, you stood a good chance of having your leg broken, but I never saw this happen. In the early hours of the morning, one would crawl back to one's tent, providing it had been left standing, bruised, battered and sore, often clothes torn and stained, but serenely happy, having well and truly got rid of all the superfluous energy, and dreading the bugle call, only too soon, for reveille.

There was of course, one exception. This was the orderly officer, dressed in his patrols, Sam Browne and sword, which he was required to remove immediately on entering the mess. His job was to mount the ceremonial guard and fire picket at 6 p.m. each evening. This was quite an event, and the R.S.M. would often walk down to the parade ground to observe and also to see whether the orderly officer made any mistakes

The officers of the Kent/Sussex Brigade of the Royal Artillery Territorial Army at camp in 1938.

A 6 inch gun for practice at Culver Isle of Wight.

in his drill. If he did so, he would be informed firmly but politely, of the error of his ways. We were, in fact, as apprehensive of the R.S.M. as we were of the adjutant. The orderly officer would select the stick man from the guard. This was the best and smartest turned out gunner. The honour was somewhat dubious, as it was the duty of the stick man to run any errands for the guard for the rest of his tour of duty, but I have no doubt it had its own perks, of which we were not aware. It was the duty of the orderly officer to turn out the guard at least once during the night; usually about 2 a.m. was the selected time. During the day, he would meet up with the orderly sergeant, and together they would inspect the whole camp. They would visit the latrines and ensure that the army form blank, the traditional term for toilet paper, was in sufficient supply, they would visit the tent lines to ensure their tidiness, the cookhouse to ensure its cleanliness, and at meal times, again visit the dining marquee, to enquire whether there were any complaints. There seldom were, and there was often some good natured chatter. He would also visit the sergeants' mess, being very careful to remove his headdress before entering the tent. There he would be invited to take a little liquid refreshment, ostensibly to ensure that the beer was fit for human consumption. We usually had about two tours of duty as orderly officer, and the job was by no means onerous. It all formed part of our training for the big event to come — fighting the Germans! Once during the camp period, it was traditional for the R.S.M. to invite the officers over to the sergeants' mess. This was always a very liquid occasion, during which the sergeants tried to prove that they were better drinkers than the officers. Pints of beer were provided in an endless stream, and the sergeants usually proved their point. Tradition demanded that the sergeants were never invited back to the officers' mess, which I felt was a bit unfair.

We had two camps at Yaverland before the war, in 1937 and 1938, but in 1939 it was ordered that our camp was to be taken at our war stations in Dover. It was a bit disappointing to have to remain in our home town, in a field behind Langdon Battery, but quite logical really, as we would now be training in the location and on the weapons we would man in the time of war.

In addition to the annual camp, I had the audacity in March, 1938 to approach my employers once again, to enquire whether I might attend a T.A. Subalterns' course at the School of Gunnery at Shoeburyness. To my surprise this was granted, but of course would count as my annual leave. I thought this would be the quickest way to learn my job, or hobby as I then regarded it.

The course was well conducted and planned, and we were expected to work hard. Our instructors were polite, helpful and understanding. They probably realised they were dealing with enthusiastic amateurs, who had given up their holidays to try and learn a little about gunnery. They were always willing to give up their spare time after classes, to go over again one of their lectures, and give the less initiated, like myself, extra tuition. I greatly admired their patience and helpfulness, and envied them their vast knowledge. I repaid them by making the biggest blunder on the course. It took place during a night shoot from the four 12 pounders, sited on a gantry, below the 6 inch guns. These four guns were all in a line and manned entirely by officers, with the assistant instructor gunners, in their traditional white trousers and navy blue jackets, behind each gun, to watch the drill and give advice where needed. My particular job that night was No. 2, whose task it was to open and close the breech. When the gun fired, I was supposed to open the breech and with a tool, extract the spent brass cartridge, to enable the loading numbers to insert a new shell and cartridge. The layer was supposed to fire the gun, after I had closed the breech and called 'Ready'. Usually a keen layer, to increase the rate of fire, would keep his finger hard pressed against the gun trigger mechanism, so that the gun fired as soon as the breech was closed, and the No. 2 had to be very snappy to get his hand free of the breech, otherwise he would get a nasty bang on the knuckles, as the gun recoiled. The noise when all four guns fired together, was tremendous. I closed the breech, yelled 'Ready', and there was the usual very loud explosion. I immediately assumed my gun had fired, so I whipped open the breech, and extracted what I thought was the spent brass cartridge. The loading number, immediately inserted another shell, but when he came to ram home the cartridge, he could only get it halfway in. We all looked a bit dumbfounded, until the A.I.G. rushed up to see what the trouble was. It did not take him long to find out that I had in fact extracted a live cartridge, throwing it to the ground, and then the loading No. 2, believing the gun had fired, had rammed home another shell. The A.I.G., with a rather red face, informed me that I had been responsible for the gun being 'double shotted' and the cartridge I had hurled with gay abandon to the rear, could easily have exploded, and blown us all to kingdom come. It was quite a business extracting both the rammed shells. There was no danger as they were only sand-filled but a long pole had to be pushed down from the muzzle end to force both shells out through the breech, whilst we just stood around, feeling very foolish. By the time the shells were extracted, the shoot was all over.

I was always amused, at Shoeburyness, to see after a shoot and at low water, a horse and cart go forth to pick up the expended sand-filled shells, and return them, if not too damaged, for use again, in the interests of economy.

When the course had been completed, a report on one's progress was sent, first to the officer commanding Fixed Defences, Eastern Ports, and then on to the adjutant, who noted it carefully. One then had to report to the adjutant, who read out the report to the individual. I never heard of anyone receiving a really bad report in peacetime, from Shoeburyness, but nevertheless, one always reported with some apprehension, as a bad report could well mean a discharge from the army. It was the general remarks by the colonel commanding the Coast Artillery School, and one's position on the course, and examination result, which really concerned one. I wondered if my double shotting would count heavily against me, and that I would be told that I was useless as a gunner. On glancing through my scrapbook, I found my old certificate which read as follows: —

Position on course   9/18   Marks gained in exam   74%
Remarks by C.O., C.A. School
'Showed great keenness and did well on course.'

As I have written earlier, they were very kind to young Territorial officers in peacetime. I suppose, on reflection, this result was not too bad, and I was at least half way. I wonder however what the I.G.'s and A.I.G.'s really thought about it all. Perhaps after all they were in fact sorry for the amateurs, who had given up their holidays to try and learn something and not make such a fool of themselves in front of the old gunners and sweats. Sometimes I think they must have been at bursting point, and it is to their eternal credit that they showed such patience, considering what they were confronted with.

5 *The first warning*

And so the training of the volunteers continued. We had one object in view. This was to pass the Certificate in Gunnery. For this we would be required to appear before a board of senior officers and select any gun of our choice. We would then be closely examined and questioned on the equipment, and be expected to satisfy the officers that we knew our job and could carry out our duties with competence. We were also expected to have a thorough knowledge of the equipment, and its functions and workings. If we could not satisfy the board, it could request our resignation. I selected the 12 pounder and am happy to say that I managed to squeeze through. There was no written report; the board merely informed you that it was satisfied as to your efficiency, and that training was to continue with enthusiasm and fervour.

Suddenly there was a rude shock — September, 1938. Nothing was farther from my mind, when there was a knock on my front door. There stood a member of the permanent staff from Liverpool Street Drill Hall at 5 o'clock one afternoon, requesting that I immediately put together my small kit, get into uniform, notify my employers that I would not be turning up for duty the following day, and then report to the Liverpool Street Drill Hall as quickly as possible and certainly no later than 30 minutes hence. Fortunately I lived on the Dover seafront, only a short distance away, but our architect captain, who lived in London, had to get a taxi down. Our battery commander, being his own boss and aware that the balloon was likely to go up, had spent the last couple of days in the Drill Hall. Naturally, from the newspapers, I was aware that the Prime Minister was on his way to Munich, and that fellow Hitler had been making a lot of noise and trouble, but it had not occurred to me that war was just around the corner. The P.S.I., civilian clerks, and police were all tearing around Dover, either to places of employment or private houses, informing the members of the regiment that they were all mobilised, and to get down to their respective drill halls, Dover, Ramsgate, Lewes and Brighton, as soon as possible. And so it had happened: we were now all soldiers and no longer civilians in uniform. When I arrived at the Drill Hall, the B.C. informed me that, as soon as about a dozen men reported in, I was to go to the end of the Eastern Arm, prepare the two 12 pounders for action, and generally get things organised until the main body of men arrived. I enquired, somewhat

A view of the end of the Eastern Arm showing the searchlight aperture. This photograph was taken before the 1914-18 war as it shows no aerial coal transporter system whose dust caused extra problems for those manning the Eastern Arm defences. The eastern docks appear to be under construction. Note the tents on Langdon cliff.

timidly, what I should fire at, and was told to point the loaded guns in the direction of the enemy, and to fire at anything, which in my opinion, committed an hostile act. Well, we all went off, about ten in my car and the remainder on bicycles. The Eastern Arm gateman looked a bit askance when a bunch of T.A. soldiers came through to the Arm at this hour—it was then about 6 p.m., and on this day of the week. But we rushed through, now feeling rather important, and it seemed it was all developing into one big joke.

When we arrived, as there was an insufficient number of men to have a manning parade, we all went up to the battery store room to draw all the necessary equipment and breeches, etc. The district gunner (there was one appointed to each battery, to maintain all the stores and ensure the equipment was in good working order) was already there. Fortunately somebody had had the presence of mind to mobilise the civilian district gunners, although in fact our own B.S.M. was employed as a district gunner and lived with his wife and family of young children along the Admiralty Pier, in quarters immediately below the 6 inch guns and adjoining the turret containing the old 81 tonners. He used to keep a board setting out the history of the old guns, and I believe would show visitors around on request.

Returning to the manning of the Eastern Arm, having more or less got everything ready and some live ammunition up from the magazine, which incidentally was the first time I had actually handled it, I decided

*Another early photo
showing the quarters
used by the R.A.T.A.
at the end of the
Eastern Arm.*

that the guns should have a look-out bearing in the general direction of
Germany. I was uncertain in which direction Germany lay. It seemed
wrong just to point them out to sea, as they would then be pointing in the
direction of France, who was now an ally. So we directed them straight
up the Channel. If there was to be a surprise attack on the port, it must
surely come from the east. We then sat down to await the arrival of more
men and our battery captain, hurrying in his taxi from London. There
was a telephone operating directly to the castle and now I noticed
unusual naval activity within the port itself. Many more buoys were
being anchored in the harbour in anticipation of the arrival of more
ships, and work was in progress on an enormous contraption of wooden
blocks and chains, which later turned out to be a boom. Also there were
many more naval officers about, doing I knew not what, but obviously
engaged in numerous duties connected with the port. We were not the
only people mobilised, therefore, and I was aware that the Territorial
anti-aircraft battery, in the seafront drill hall, had been called up at the
same time as ourselves.

I suddenly realised that on the Eastern Arm, we had no food, accommodation or means of preparing for any long stay. There were some small damp rooms in the side of the Arm, perhaps big enough for a small office, one toilet and one or two fresh water taps. Beyond that there was nothing, not even a war shelter for the men on watch. There were one or two other rooms, but these were occupied by the navy and Dover Harbour Board personnel, then responsible for the control of the entry and departure of shipping. Fortunately it was a fine night, and nobody seemed to want to sleep, which was just as well as there was nowhere to sleep anyway. I telephoned the very harassed quartermaster, who promised he would do his best and send us up a mobile stove for heating water, some buckets, pots, mugs and anything else he thought may be useful until he could get things organised. He did not, however, have any food to send us and said the men should have brought sufficient rations from their homes to last them 24 hours. I do not think it had occurred to anyone to make such a provision. He said he could not come out and build us a hut, but arrangements were in hand for the Southern Railway to shunt a couple of railway coaches along the Arm and we could use those. I found a small room leading off the magazine, which in the first war had been an old searchlight emplacement and provided an excellent view across the eastern entrance. We could use this as an office, mess and sleeping quarters for the two officers. The remaining rooms we would allocate to the men, until the arrival of the promised railway coaches. But the cookhouse, provided there was anything to cook, would have to be in the open for the time being. A few more men drifted in and the battery captain had arrived. We were then able to divide ourselves into watches and await developments.

It was a fine clear night and the off duty watch slept out on the concrete on sacks they had found lying about. There were no complaints from anybody, and it all seemed a little unreal. There was no blackout and everything in the town was, no doubt, going along quite normally. Our bosses were probably irritated by our non-arrival at our offices, buses, shops and places of business and some people were inconvenienced by our absence. But then, after all, we were being a bit inconvenienced ourselves. Next morning, the B.C. and I, with our only means of transport, my old car, decided to pool our cash resources. Until the R.H.Q. had got themselves sorted out, it was unlikely we would get much help from that direction. The R.Q.M.S. had kept his promise and sent out all the things we had asked for, except food. So it was decided that with the help of a bombardier, and all the cash we could muster between us, I set off in my car to the International Stores, then situated in the Market Square. There we bought bread, butter, eggs, tea, cocoa, cereals and milk to the limit of my cash resources, piled it into the car and returned triumphant. I felt a bit self-conscious, in uniform buying groceries, when by rights I should have been at work but there was nothing I nor anyone else could do about it.

We next appointed a cook, a volunteer who said he had some knowledge of cooking and would do his best. He was in fact a miner from Tilmanstone colliery. It is interesting to note at this stage that in later years, he passed all examinations at the Army Catering School at Aldershot and became a sergeant class I cook. It was with no such thoughts in his mind, that he undertook to distribute our rations and get his Sawyer stove working. Somehow we were all fed, picnic style, and it all seemed a lot of fun and quite an adventure, We provided the naval personnel with some amusement, and if this was war, it was not going to be too bad. The only thing missing was the Germans, and if they had arrived, I am sure we would have invited them to join us in our gay repast.

However, it was not long before things became more organised and assumed a military air. By mid-day, a truck arrived from Langdon with more blankets and our initial supply of rations. The navy kindly lent us some coal to keep the stove burning. The O.C. arrived to see that we had not all got fed up and gone home, and informed us that we were as well off as all the other batteries and probably better off than most. Brighton had arrived and were manning Langdon and South Breakwater 6 inch guns and Ramsgate were safely installed in Pier Turret and Pier Extension. 168 Battery, Dover, were manning the Citadel 9.2 guns whilst 30 of us were on the Eastern Arm. R.H.Q. was still in the Liverpool Street Drill Hall and the Fire Command Post, our operational H.Q. was manned by regular soldiers under a major. The adjutant arrived soon after the departure of the B.C. with a pile of army forms with a variety of numbers, which were quite meaningless to us. The army always seemed to refer to its form and returns by the number on the form. It seemed to assume that everybody was fully conversant with a jargon of numbers instead of referring to the form itself. The adjutant instructed us to familiarise ourselves with army administration which had to go on, war or no war. We must calculate our daily rations and indent for them, at least three days before they were to be consumed, giving the exact number of persons who would consume them. If somebody was posted in or out during those three days, it was just too bad, and adjustments then had to be made later on a subsequent form. We had to indent for beds, although we had no place to put them, but this was on the schedule, and numerous other items, some we would need, whilst others were of no use at all and in fact would only be in the way. But it was laid down in some manual or other that this was the issue, and this we had to have. The ammunition had to be carefully checked and counted, and placed in batches according to age, and the gun history sheet which records the number of rounds and type fired had to be studied so that wear on the barrel could be recorded and allowed for. Although the magazine was fitted with electric light, there were a number of recesses in the walls in which stood large Victorian type lamps, containing candles. One had to ensure that all the candles were of different lengths, to be certain that in an emergency, when the electricity failed, and the candles had to be lighted, they did not all go out at the same time. I wonder who the army genius was who thought this one up.

Officers were now excused the wearing of spurs, although we still looked rather strange at the end of the Eastern Arm in our riding breeches and field boots, and not a horse in sight. The harbour itself had

Opposite
Langdon Battery in 1938.

now assumed a very active role. Destroyers were rushing in and out and supply ships appeared to revictual all their needs. Some minesweepers appeared and a very business-like atmosphere settled all round the area. However, it still seemed rather unrealistic to see the cross-channel vessels, using the eastern entrance only, still running according to their published timetable, and still carrying passengers and holiday makers to numerous resorts for holidays on the continent.

And so we stayed for about another ten days, muddling our way along, all rather confused, but nevertheless taking advantage of what we considered a prolonged training period, for which we were being paid. We wrote to our families and we wrote to our employers, and from the publicity in the papers, we were not held up to ridicule. Some people realised that there was a Territorial Army, who was prepared to take its place in defence of the country, and playing at soldiers was not just a silly pastime, but was now something to be reckoned with. I well recollect that during the period September, 1938 to August 1939, our recruiting figures gave an upward jump, and many more volunteers came forward in every branch of the services.

Mr. Chamberlain returned in about ten days from Munich, clutching a piece of paper saying, 'Peace in our time', but I am sure few really believed him. It meant to us the order 'Replace stores', pack up all our things and next morning to report back to our civilian jobs. I half expected some ridicule, but surprisingly it was not forthcoming. Everyone had had rather a fright, and seemed relieved that it was now over, at least for the time being. As far as we were concerned, it had been a good excercise in mobilisation and we had profited by it. Many weaknesses had been revealed, and steps were taken to remedy some of them, where it was possible to do so, should we be mobilised again. For instance, the railway coaches were now a firm commitment, by the Southern Railway, who promised to shunt them along immediately they were required, and in fact did so in 1939.

Lewis guns for drill purposes only had been replaced by more serviceable weapons. Training in passive air defence was intensified, but we still had no effective means, other than rifles, for protecting ourselves against low flying air attack.

So we went back to our weekly training, content in the knowledge that the defence of Dover was in good hands and the good citizens of the town had nothing to fear and could sleep soundly in their beds at night — or could they?

6 Off we go again

After a further fortnight's camp in July, during which much of our time was occupied in the preparation and shoot off for the King's Cup, we found ourselves faced with another call-up within 12 months. On 22nd August, 1939, the regiment was mobilised again. We imagined it would be for another fortnight, although this time, in our heart of hearts, we knew it would be the real thing.

We had profited by our experience the previous year, and this time I was detailed for duty at the Citadel Battery. The equipment there was much the same, although the Magslip dials on slip rings did away with the old testing of Watkin dials, and all the trouble they had caused. The equipment on the Eastern Arm, however, had been changed or rather was in the process of being changed. The 12 pounder guns had been removed and in their place now stood the latest and most efficient anti-motor torpedo boat gun. I believe this was the first operational equipment in the country, although Shoeburyness had for some little time been training on a similar type of gun. Each equipment consisted of a double-barreled 6 pounder gun, called a 'twin six' and could fire 72 rounds per minute, with a hosepipe effect on approaching fast moving craft. Workmen were still engaged in building two towers, one behind each equipment to enable the ranging to be carried out by means of a director, which transmitted ranges and bearings to Magslip dials on the equipment below. The layers on the gun floor were merely required to match the pointer controlled by him and connected with the gun traversing and elevation gears, with a movable arm on the dial. The towers, which stood about 30 feet high, not only provided additional height for the director layers, but ensured that they were not unsighted by the pall of smoke which usually formed in front of each equipment, after a few rounds had been fired, blinding the auto-sight and line layers trying to peer through their telescopes. In addition, at the top of each tower, a small platform was provided to fix a Lewis gun and later a Bren gun for A.A. protection.

Work on the towers had only just commenced when we arrived again in 1939 and we had had no prolonged training on the equipment. Although the 6 pounders were ready for action, the concrete emplacements were not yet finished and they were supported by a wooden gantry. There were concrete mixers, cement sacks, dust and

The Gun Batteries defending Dover

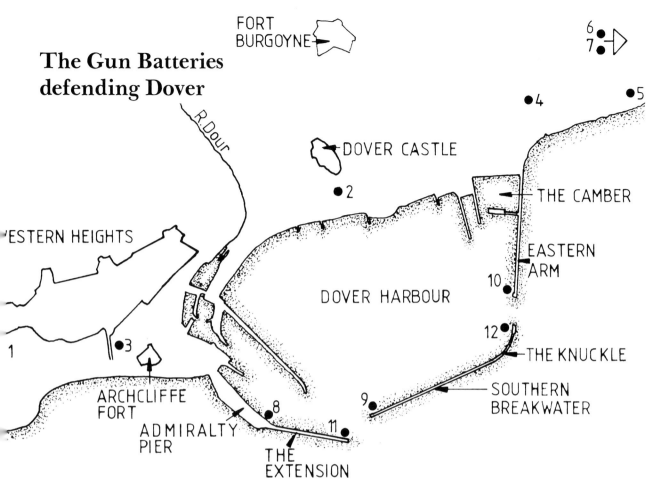

FORT BURGOYNE

R.Dour

DOVER CASTLE

●2

●4

●5

6●
7●

THE CAMBER

EASTERN ARM

●10

'ESTERN HEIGHTS

DOVER HARBOUR

●12

THE KNUCKLE

1

●3

SOUTHERN BREAKWATER

ARCHCLIFFE FORT

ADMIRALTY PIER

●8

9●

●11

THE EXTENSION

cement wash everywhere and it was not easy to keep the guns clean and dust free. There was still no sleeping accommodation, and the war shelter was still only half built. Very shortly, however, as promised, two railway carriages arrived and were shunted into the battery. The compartments were not modified in any way, but they provided shelter from the elements and often times slept no fewer than ten men to a single compartment. Others found the cement sacks a little softer under the large coal bunker, where wooden huts were being erected, together with a cookhouse. At present the cook still worked in the open with his sawyer stove, and somehow provided meals for the whole battery by the most primitive methods. Life was made a little more uncomfortable by the appearance of a large number of rats, and they could sometimes be seen in swarms advancing up the Arm. They were not a pretty sight, and on one occasion, whilst sleeping in our small concrete shelter, I was awakened by a large rat landing on my chest. The B.C. offered a small monetary reward for every rat-tail exhibited, and I strongly believe he paid out more than once on the same tail!

Similar arrangements for Pier Turret Battery and Pier extension existed, although I believe a number of men found shelter in the Marine Station. Pier Turret was a little better off than the Eastern Arm. They had the district gunner's quarters as he had now removed his family to a

1 Citadel Battery.
2 Fire Command Post and P.W.S.S.
3 St. Martins Battery.
4 Langdon Battery.
5 Fan Bay Battery.
6 Wanstone Battery.
7 South Foreland Battery.
8 Pier Turret Battery.
9 South Breakwater Battery.
10 Eastern Arm Battery.
11 Pier Extention Battery.
12 Knuckle Battery.

safer and more comfortable surround, and they also had the old turret of the 81 tonners, which had a dry wooden floor. The Southern Breakwater, like the Eastern Arm, had a few small rooms let into the mole, but they were insufficient to house the battery, although similar accommodation had been used in the first war. Anyway it was impossible to give them railway trucks, and so they had to make do. Contrary to popular belief, there is no passageway between either the Admiralty Pier or the Eastern Arm, and it is only possible to reach the Southern Breakwater by boat. The Citadel battery was probably the best accommodated battery. Not only were there one or two suitable small huts, but a vast area of accommodation opened up in the casemates and old moat, which had the additional advantage of providing excellent air raid shelters. Langdon Battery also, whilst it had insufficient and primitive accommodation, had the barracks nearby, and could manage moderately well, until the garrison engineer, that very hard-pressed and harassed man, could build more wooden huts to the rear of the guns. Many men at Langdon preferred to sleep in the magazines, beneath the guns, but such accommodation was not looked upon too favourably, as there was always a danger if anyone started smoking.

Artillery surrounding the town for seaward protection in 1939 consisted of two 9.2 guns at the Citadel, two 6 inch guns halfway along the Admiralty Pier, now known as Pier Turret Battery, two 12 pounders at the end of the Admiralty Pier, now known as Pier Extension Battery, and two 6 inch guns on the Southern Breakwater, now known as Breakwater Battery. (It is interesting to note that the breakwater or central mole was about 4000 feet long and 40 feet wide and the battery was sited at the extreme west side of the mole). There were two 6 inch guns at Langdon Battery, designated the Examination Battery and finally two twin six pounder equipments at the end of the Eastern Arm, which was obliged to assume the examination role in foggy weather. In addition, coast artillery searchlights were allotted, two fighting lights to each 6 inch, five searchlights at the end of the Eastern Arm and Knuckle, with wide dispersal beams, and a further five searchlights of similar kind covering the western entrance of the harbour. These provided an illuminated area in front of both entrances to facilitate the engagement of fast moving craft, which could not be followed by a fighting light. In all there were 16 searchlights and four engine-rooms to supply the power. The engines were mainly Lister, and later Ruston Hornby. The tactical control of both guns and lights were in the hands of Fire Commander, in a control post sited on the cliff edge in front of Cliff Block, the administrative headquarters of the regiment in 1940. Immediately above the fire command post was housed the Naval Port War Signal Station, which by means of flag and signal lamp could communicate with all ships in the harbour and any in the vicinity or approaching. The flag post above the P.W.S.S. indicated the state of air alert — red, green or yellow, red indicating immediate attack, yellow, a precautionary warning, and green, all clear. There was a direct communication between the P.W.S.S. and the F.C. post by telephone and voice tube, and the F.C. had direct lines to all batteries and coast artillery. Later of course, when the C.A. operations room had been set up, the tactical control was taken over by the corps commander and lines installed between all the F.C. posts and radar stations.

The fire command post was also equipped with a visual depression rangefinder, similar to a position finder, to enable him to measure range and bearing to a possible target and note its map reference. To obtain such a reference, the sea area all around the coast was divided into squares, called block, square and point. By passing on block, square and point to a battery, both could be sure they were looking at the same target. The fire commander also had attached to him a naval commander, called an extended defence officer, to advise on the nationality and type of warship, within visual range of the port. The duties of the X.D.O. were later extended to the operation of the controlled minefields, later laid across both entrances. The drill between

Opposite
The Battery Observation Post built on the Eastern Arm.
Lewis gunners gave protection from low flying aircraft.

F.C. and P.W.S.S. was quite a simple one. When a vessel approached the harbour, and having given the correct signal, the P.W.S.S. would inform the F.C. that the vessel was friendly and requested permission to enter harbour. The F.C. would then call up all batteries in rotation, and inform them that the vessel was friendly. Having obtained their acknowledgements, the F.C. would inform the P.W.S.S. that the vessel had permission to enter. It seems a long drawn-out procedure but in practice, took very little time. The battery telephones were manned 24 hours a day and the F.C. telephonist would pass over the message once, and every battery would acknowledge in a matter of seconds. If a battery failed to reply or kept the F.C. telephonist waiting, if only for a couple of seconds, a roar would go up and the battery telephonist given a sound wigging.

If there were a direct attack upon the harbour, it was the duty of the fire commander to fight off the enemy by correct employment of the batteries, according to a pre-arranged plan. This plan, drawn up by the fire commander, and approved by the corps commander, was known as 'Fire Commander's Standing Orders for Dover Fire Command'. It was contained in a top secret file, and every battery signed for a copy. It was an accountable document, and marked 'Top Secret'. Woebetide any B.C. who could not produce it immediately on request and more important still, did not have all the amendments stuck in. Of course he had to know the S.O.'s off almost by heart.

They contained the following information: —

A detailed Distribution of Fire Scheme.
Rules for opening fire.
Traffic control procedure.
States of readiness.
Organisation of watches and reliefs.
Coast artillery searchlights.
Choice of projectiles.
Forms of likely attack.
Synchronisation of watches.
Tide tables.
Official Day and Night.
Royal Naval responsibilities.
Ground defence schemes.
Communications.
Passive Air Defence.
Probable enemy objectives.
Landwards firing.
Pyrotechnic signals.

The orders carried many more instructions and the above are but a few things the battery commanders were required to know. They were allowed to make their own note books or fighting books as they are called, on a number of points, particular to their own batteries.

To gain a clear insight on how the town and port were to be defended in the event of a naval attack or invasion, it is well to study the system in a little more detail.

The types of attack envisaged on the port and fortress were outlined as follows: —

(a) The landing of small parties with the object of damaging installations and defence works.

(b) Low flying air attacks.

(c) A major military attack from the landwards side.

(d) Paratroop attack.

(e) An attack on the port by a combined fleet of major and minor war vessels.

It was decided that the western entrance be closed permanently, by the sinking of blockships and the erection of a permanent boom, and an anti-motor torpedo boat boom laid down across the eastern entrance, to be operated by a naval officer stationed at the end of the arm — a boom defence officer. The boom was made up of very large rectangular blocks, with spikes on each block, and an iron curtain beneath the blocks to prevent the passage of small submerged submarines or torpedoes.

The rules for opening fire were now made a little clearer. During day time, fire would not be opened up, unless ordered by the fire commander, except in the failure of communications. B.C.'s would open fire on their own responsibility on any unidentified submarine, on which he had not been notified, or an obvious hostile vessel within range.

During the night, B.C.'s would open fire on any war vessel which was unidentified, or which had not been notified, or on any unidentified vessel attempting to reach the shore.

The guns on the Eastern Arm. A destroyer leaving Dover Harbour, seen through the searchlight aperture on the Eastern Arm. This room was used as the officers' mess — note the beer bottles!

Fire would not be opened without the F.C.'s orders on vessels, (other than war vessels) which were not obviously hostile. On general alarm, all guns would be instantly loaded , and all C.A.S.L.'s exposed.

In the event of naval action taking place within the range of the Dover defences, fire could not be opened if it was considered it would hamper the action of our own war vessels.

I felt that we had at last come a long way since the days of Hubert de Burgh or even the rather haphazard days of 1938. Our orders were now clearly defined, but it still boiled down to the fact that it was up to the B.C. to use his own initiative in every case, which after all, was only right and proper.

The distribution of fire scheme was extremely important in the defence of the port. It was decided to employ a system of combined zone and sequence. The sea area in front of the port was divided into three zones by imaginary lines running from the centre of the Breakwater and from the Knuckle. The three areas were lettered from the east — A, B and

Above
The 81-ton gun on
the Admiralty Pier.
Opposite
Pier Turret Battery,
partially demolished
in 1958.

C, and the sea area so divided would be as follows: —

A — 164°-268°
B — 120°-164°
C — 055°-120°

It was considered that the enemy approach could be over a wide area, and his formation and direction of movement so varied, that only by the adoption of a zone system, supplemented by a sequence system, could he be effectively engaged.

If larger types of enemy vessels attempted to enter the harbour, they could only do so in line ahead through a comparatively narrow entrance and on a westerly course. They would have to run this course for at least 1000 yards before entering the harbour. The principle laid down was, all vessels would be engaged simultaneously to the limit of the guns available, the most dangerous vessel would be engaged first, and as a general rule, escorted vessels were to be considered more dangerous than their escorts. A vessel making for the harbour entrance was potentially more dangerous than one making for the beach outside.

It was decided, therefore, that the defence of the port could best be effected by a distribution of fire scheme for the eastern approaches as follows: —

LANGDON BATTERY — 6 inch guns.
No. 1 gun (Right-hand gun) will be lettered A
No. 2 gun (Left-hand gun) will be lettered B
EASTERN ARM BATTERY — Twin 6 pounders.
No. 1 Equipment (Right-hand guns) will be lettered C
No. 2 Equipment (Left-hand guns) will be lettered D
As far as the western approaches were concerned
SOUTH BREAKWATER BATTERY — 6 inch guns.
No. 1 gun (Left-hand gun) will be lettered A
No. 2 gun (Right-hand gun) will be lettered B
PIER EXTENSION BATTERY — 12 pounder guns.
No. 1 gun (Right-hand gun) will be lettered C
No. 2 gun (Left-hand gun) will be lettered D

PIER TURRET BATTERY — 6 inch guns.

No. 1 gun (Right-hand gun) will be lettered A or
C — whichever able to bear.

No. 2 gun (Left-hand gun) will be lettered B or D — whichever able to
bear.

If the enemy vessels approached in line ahead, they would be lettered
by classes in the order in which they appear, in other words, A gun
engages A target, B gun engages B target. All targets to retain their
original letters throughout the engagement.

If on the other hand, the attacking vessels approach in line abreast,
they would be lettered from right to left.

A Zone would be the secondary target for Pier Extension Battery, whose
primary zone would be B.

B Zone would be the primary zone of South Breakwater Battery.

C Zone would be the primary zone of Pier Turret Battery.

A Zone would be the primary zone of Langdon and Eastern Arm.

South Breakwater would normally be required to support A Zone
unless engaged in action in B Zone.

The first gun to sink or disable a target would then direct its fire on the
next unengaged target.

The rules, when first studied might seem complicated and confusing,
but in fact, they were only common sense. When practised a few times
with models, their employment by the batteries became fairly
straightforward. It would have been easy for everyone to start firing at
vessels as they presented themselves, and in this way, it would have been
possible for an enemy to get close, if not enter the harbour, without a
shot being fired at him.

Later, when Fan Bay guns came into operation, they were obviously
alloted to A Zone, and the scheme amended accordingly.

Citadel Battery did not enter the distribution of fire scheme for the
defence of the port, but was required by the navy to engage the heavier
and leading ship.

In point of fact, no such major attack on Dover took place, but if it
had done so, it would then have been too late to organise the most
effective defence. The scheme ensured that the maximum amount of fire
power could be used for the defence of the port. With the number of
guns available, it was vital that none should be idle during an attack.
The fighting lights were given areas of search, defined within certain arcs
and degrees. The Langdon fighting lights were sited on a concrete wall,
at the base of the cliff, some 10 feet above high water, and could only be
approached by a small zig-zag path down the cliff from Langdon Hole,
outside the battery perimeter.

A manual was published by the navy, setting out the responsibilities
for traffic control, and giving instructions for the examination service
and entry into British ports in time of war.

A means of identification of friendly ships was required, and
accordingly an examination anchorage, both inner and outer was
defined, and the anchorage patrolled by an examination vessel, watched
over by an examination battery. The sea area was selected off Langdon

and the battery then given the required role. Initially, a Dover Harbour Board tug was given this duty, but later a trawler was given the job.

The examination service was an integral part of the defence of the port, and certain signals and procedures had to be closely followed if a friendly vessel was not to be engaged or sunk, or alternatively an enemy vessel, under false colours be allowed to approach the port for purposes such as minelaying in the approaches, or entry for far more devastating acts.

First there was the private signal. This was used by principal classes of the R.N. and convoys and could be used by allied war vessels. The signal changed daily, in accordance with secret keys issued to all the major war vessels. It was always visual or sound and never by wireless.

The major war vessel or the convoys would always be required to notify the P.W.S.S. of their expected time of arrival, and if later by 15 minutes a further message would have to be sent. On arrival the usual challenge was made by P.W.S.S. with interrogative pennant, and a reply would be made by the display of the private signal, by lamp at night or by sound in fog. The usual procedure, as already described, was then followed with the fire commander and batteries.

The examination service itself was in no way connected with vessels flying the private signal. The service had two procedures for entry: —

Ship to Shore Signal

This was visual and changed at fixed periods, two or three times a day. It was mainly used by minor war vessels and coastal forces. It was the responsibility of the vessel to fly the correct pennants by day or series of lights by night, otherwise a 'bring to' round would be fired and this happened on numerous occasions. Vessels would not display the signal correctly or display a signal which was out of date, sometimes by only 10 minutes.

Special Signal

This was again visual and used by merchantmen other than in convoy. When independent shipping arrived near the port, it was examined by the examination vessel. If the X.V. was satisfied as to the identity of the vessel and her cargo, she would be given the special signal and could then proceed to enter the port, sometimes with the assistance of a local pilot. If however, the X.V. was not satisfied, she would order the vessel to the inner anchorage, notify the examination battery, who would keep the vessel covered. The X.V. would possibly put aboard an armed party and make a more thorough examination until such time as she was ready to give the vessel the special signal. If the vessel attempted to move from the inner anchorage, a bring to round was immediately fired, and if she did not then stop, she would be sunk.

On no occasion did such an incident occur. Many vessels were closely examined and then allowed to enter the harbour, but the enemy at no time attempted to use this ruse to cause damage to the port. Many bring to rounds were fired, some I fear a little too freely. At the examination battery at Langdon, young officers would vie with one another on who could fire the most number of 'bring to's' in a week. A round was fired at a very familiar local sight, on one occasion. This was the poor old pilot cutter, who happened to be only five minutes late in changing her signal, and she was made to retreat out into the Channel again. This was due entirely to the over-zealousness of a subaltern on duty in the battery, wishing to increase his score of bring to rounds. On one occasion I brought the wrath of the navy on my own shoulders. Whilst on duty at the Eastern Arm, and having been instructed to take over examination duties owing to foggy weather, I saw approaching a patrol vessel. Visibility was not good and although she was flying a signal, due to the angle of her approach, it was quite impossible to distinguish. It would, in my opinion be foolish to allow the vessel to enter, if I could not be certain as to her identity, and accordingly I fired a 'bring to' round. As she was approaching head on, I fired slightly to her starboard, but sufficiently close for her watch keeping officer to observe. She immediately swung round to starboard, and as a consequence, I was able to see her signal clearly, and determine that it was a perfectly correct one. The P.W.S.S. came to the rescue, and sent her a visual signal to enter port. By a strange coincidence, I went ashore that night and called at the old Grand Hotel for a drink. There I met two naval officers, who informed me in quite forcible naval language, that I had a colleague on the Eastern Arm who thought he was William Tell. I did not have the courage to inform them that it was I, but I did buy them a drink and we parted in a friendly manner.

This, then, was the full procedure drawn up by the Royal Navy and Army authorities for the defence of Dover, and the contents of these standing orders were constantly being taught on drill nights, by lectures and instruction with the use of models made of wood. It was essential that we mastered the distribution of fire scheme, both in daylight and under night conditions.

The examination service did not concern us greatly as it seemed straightforward enough, and we gave no attention to any reference to landwards firing, for who could possibly imagine that our beloved guns would ever have to point to an enemy behind us? The idea that anyone, including Hitler, should ever entertain the idea that he could invade Britain, was inconceivable. If we went to war, he might try an attack with his pocket battleships and destroyers, and we rather hoped he would, but beyond that our training did not allow for any more adventurous move on his part.

Furthermore we never imagined that a situation would arise whereby the enemy would bombard us from the French coast, and certainly those in authority did not think so either, as we were given no weapons then that would reach anywhere near the French shores. We had not been to war with France for well over a century. They were now our allies, and if they allowed the Germans to reach the Calais cliffs, it would mean that the British Army also had been defeated. It was quite impossible to assimilate such a thought, and it certainly never entered our heads in the days of 1938 and 1939.

7 And so we went to war

It was on the 22nd August, 1939 that orders were received by the adjutant that the regiment was to be fully mobilised. The P.S.I.'s went forth, first to call up the 'key men'. When these had been assembled at the drill hall, they were immediately dispatched on bicycles and any other means of transport, to all the other members of the unit. To their homes, offices, to the factories, to the shops. And so they came, like Chaucer's pilgrims, from every walk and clime. The solicitors, the labourers, the accountants, the bank clerks, and the miners, the insurance clerks, and the postmen, men from Wiggins Teape paper mill, men from the Co-op, lorry drivers and bus conductors, shopkeepers and paper boys, men from the Harbour Board, an assistant registrar of births and marriages, a retired police inspector, a dustman, corporation workers and officials, publicans and postal clerks, and last but by no means least, the local doctor. All came pouring into the drill hall, whether it be Brighton, Lewes, Ramsgate, or Liverpool Street, Dover, in uniform and carrying their small kits.

As soon as about 20 men had assembled at Dover, they were dispatched to their local batteries, told to prepare for action, and later the quartermaster would arrive with some rations and blankets. Guns would be loaded, no longer with sand-filled shells, but now with high explosive. At least we were now more organised, better trained and we had our examination service, and communication with a central figure, the fire commander.

A variety of questions passed through our minds. Would we now have Lewis guns for air protection, instead of the wooden ones, on which we had trained? Would the gun dials play up and refuse to go to the appointed test points as they usually did on a Sunday morning? Would this call up be like another T.A. camp and would we really be fighting to prevent the enemy from attacking Dover, Ramsgate and Newhaven? He had to cross the sea first, and that seemed unlikely. Perhaps he would come by air and then our friends in the local anti-aircraft would deal with him. Who could tell? We had each drawn £5 mobilisation pay, which was very useful, and no doubt the family would be able to manage for the time being. And so we went to war.

On 25th August, 1939, all the batteries of the Dover defences reported to the fire commander that they were ready for action, and on 1st

September, the examination service came into being, and so the port of Dover was officially closed to merchant shipping.

On 3rd September, war was declared and this was quickly followed by a message from the fire commander and a red flag hoisted above the P.W.S.S.—air raid warning, red. We all wondered if this was to be another German blitzkreig, and although we all looked skywards, there was not an airplane of any nationality in sight. Green, or all clear, was received from the F.C. at 11.59 hours.

Perhaps another landmark, although not quite so significant, in the history of the local volunteers, was reached when orders were received on 29th September, that the wearing of 'T' on the shoulders of all Territorial officers and men was abolished, (and sadly has never returned). 'Striptease' the troops called it and they were not at all pleased, when their only distinguishing feature, setting them apart from regular soldiers, reservists, and later called-up men, disappeared. It seemed rather petty at the time, as the men were very proud of their Territorial association, but no doubt the powers that be, who sit in high authority, and supposed to be so wise in these matters, had their reasons for ordering the removal of the last emblem denoting a volunteer.

The first round to be fired, more in amusement than in anger, was fired by Langdon Battery in her examination role, on 19th October, at the trawler *Galina*, attempting to enter the western entrance. A vigorous exchange of signals took place between the trawler and the P.W.S.S., as the former had now retired into the channel to sulk, and eventually the correct signal was hoisted and she sailed in unharmed, and so peace once again was restored. I did not think, however, that we should regard this episode as the opening round of the war, as far as Dover was concerned.

Until all the local vessels became used to the new system, plugged rounds were fired nearly every day. Perhaps the first round to be fired in anger was on 12th November by Langdon Battery, quickly followed by Eastern Arm Battery. A pole was observed about 1000 yards off the end of the Eastern Arm, and could easily have been mistaken for a submarine periscope. Three rounds were fired from Langdon No. 1 gun whilst No. 2 gun could only manage one round before firing was stopped. Eastern Arm twin six made short work of the supposed periscope, which later turned out to be a paravane which had broken adrift from a minesweeper. Perhaps the most dangerous round fired by Langdon was on 6th December, 1939, when a 'bring to' round was fired at the *Twickenham Ferry,* which was approaching the harbour stern first. She was heavily laden with sea mines, and these could be seen stored along her deck. One mistake or a badly laid round by the examination battery, would not only have blown us all up but half the town as well. As it so happened, the round fell fairly close, as she was travelling quite fast at the time, and the maximum left deflection applied to the autosight, was barely sufficient. However she was flying the incorrect signal, and so must take her share of the blame.

We had our share of very important persons visiting the batteries. On 8th June, 1940, we were honoured by a visit from H.M. the King, who was visiting the fixed defences, and again King George visited us on 14th

N.R. 50.

NATIONAL REGISTER.

NATIONAL REGISTRATION DAY IS FRIDAY, 29th SEPTEMBER, 1939.

SEE INSTRUCTIONS IN SCHEDULE AS TO "PERSONS TO BE INCLUDED."

RATIONING.—The return on the schedule herewith will be used not only for National Registration but also for Food Rationing purposes. It is to your interest, therefore, as well as your public duty, to fill up the return carefully, fully and accurately.

Help the Enumerator to collect the schedule promptly by arranging for him to receive it when he calls. Do not make it necessary for him to call a number of times before he can obtain it.

When the Enumerator collects the schedule, he must write and deliver an Identity Card for every person included in the return. Help him to write them properly for you by letting him write at a table.

If the whole household moves before the schedule is collected, take it with you and hand it to the Enumerator calling at your new residence or to the National Registration Office for your new address. The address of this office can be ascertained at a local police station.

Wt 28033—171 12 50

March. Five days later, there followed a visit from Brigadier Archibald, M.C., the B.R.A. Eastern Command, and Brigadier Burrowes, O.B.E., the G.S.O. 1 Command, so we could hardly say we were being neglected. It did mean a lot of polishing and painting to get the battery in a sparkling condition for the visitors, but it was a change from the routine. The guard turnout had to be really first-class, and no doubt it was as we received the usual congratulations later.

The first drafting of the original volutcers took place on 14th February, 1940, when the 5th Kent and Sussex Super Heavy Battery was formed for duty in France. The Commanding Officer and 90 per cent of the men were Territorials from the local Regiment, and in fact there were more volunteers than there were vacancies. Replacements for the batteries soon arrived, mainly from called-up men, but the hardcore of the coastal artillery was still with the batteries and training the newcomers presented no great difficulty. The 'phoney war' was still in being and gradually a feeling was creeping over us that this was going to be just another prolonged T.A. camp. There had been no real action

The official notice of National Registration Day. The same date marked the end of volunteer soldiers. A view from the Eastern Arm showing destroyers anchored in the harbour.

and the Channel was firmly in the hands of the Allies. There had been some minelaying activity by the enemy, but we ourselves had not seen it and relied on the stories told to us by the men of the minesweepers when they came ashore. The minelaying was always carried out at night, beyond the range of our searchlights, and in those days we had no early warning from any radar set. All seemed so quiet and all our careful preparations seemed now to be a waste of time. The huts and battery surrounds were now getting to an advanced stage, so although the winter had been particularly bitter, and the men on the two moles and the central breakwater had had a fairly rough time, especially the gun lookouts, it all seemed rather fruitless. We envied our colleagues who had volunteered and been accepted for the 5th Kent & Sussex Super Heavy Regiment, and we wondered whether a further opportunity would present itself to us, to get across to France in one capacity or another, as long as we were gunners. It certainly seemed to us that Dover did not need defending, and the examination service was getting to be rather a bore, and quite farcical.

The war, as such, was brought home to us by *HMS Kittiwake,* a small minesweeper, then classified as a corvette and armed with one four inch A.A. gun. She gave chase to an enemy submarine, reported in the vicinity of the North Foreland. Relying on her shallow draft, she crossed a minefield to increase her chance of engaging the enemy, but with disastrous results. There was a violent explosion and the *Kittiwake* virtually had the middle blown out of her. She did not sink and was towed back to the harbour, and tied up alongside the Eastern Arm Battery. She had a number of casualties, wounded and dead, and it was the first time we had seen a British warship so badly damaged. A mass of twisted metal with decks blown apart, and leaving a gaping hole right amidships. This indeed, was the first tragedy, as far as we were concerned, and it made us all realise that the war was really on and that a lot of people were getting killed and hurt in the defence of their country.

We had another fright in those early days. About 2 a.m. one morning, there was a terrific explosion. A number of windows were blasted in, and one could hear all the debris crashing back on the mole. It transpired that a sea mine had broken adrift and had been swept up against the seaward side of the Arm and detonated. The noise had been colossal, and our first thoughts were that a German capital ship had opened fire on us and scored a direct hit.

A number of destroyers were now based on the port, mainly 'B' Class, and names such as *Beagle, Boadicea, Boreas, Brilliant* and *Bulldog* became a familiar sight. They were not the most modern type of destroyer, having been completed in 1931, but they were armed with four 4.7 guns and eight torpedo tubes. Their duties mainly consisted of patrolling the Channel, day and night, about 8 to 10 miles off the port, and later they were given escort duties, on the convoys which passed up and down the Channel. Their leader, Captain D, completed in 1930, was *HMS Codrington* and armed with five 4.7 guns, six smaller guns and eight torpedo tubes. She was, indeed, a fine ship with an excellent turn of

speed. She made a magnificent sight leaving harbour, and then with her helm hard over, heading westward down the Channel, with the sea breaking over her bows. She presented a most formidable picture, and was certainly the most hard working vessel in the port. She later gained distinction for being the vessel which conveyed the Dutch Crown Princess and her family from Holland to England, when the Germans invaded the Netherlands.

We had occasional 'sport' during this period in firing with small arms at sea mines which had broken adrift and had become a hazard to shipping. We could not afford to use our precious twin six pounder shells, as we had been informed that any replacement to our present stock of about 5000 rounds in the magazines was unlikely. We never fired if the mine was less than 50 yards away, as we had been informed that they contained about 750 lbs of high explosive and if they exploded too close to the battery, they could well do some damage. In these cases we

An aerial view taken on 25th February, 1941 showing the Eastern Arm in the foreground, the cliffs, Langdon Battery and Barracks (old prison), and the radar station.

65

always notified the navy, who would come out and dispose of the mine. On one occasion, however, a mine did drift unnoticed into the eastern entrance and hit the torpedo-boat boom, which fortunately happened to be closed at the time. The result was almost disastrous . A tremendous explosion blew the huge blocks of wood, studded with spikes, which formed the boom, several feet into the air, but luckily they missed the battery on landing. If they had hit us they would certainly have damaged the equipment, and we would have certainly sustained casualties. As it was, the 6 pounder ammunition was blown from the loading trolleys and loading trays and lay about the gun platform and on the concrete. Not one exploded, but the gun lookouts were badly shaken, and it improved their vigilance in the future. If, of course, the boom had been open the mine would have drifted into the harbour itself, which was crowded with shipping, and the result then could well have been calamitous.

Gradually our strength was being made up, and drafts of 50 men were being posted in mainly from the holding unit, 5th Field Training Regiment R.A. Their training on the coast guns continued, and, in fact, became even more intense. Special training rooms were set aside in each battery, and each B.C. had his own ideas on visual aids, etc. In fact there was quite a rivalry between the batteries on who could produce the best ideas and present the best training room. The Langdon Battery had the advantage of having the most space, and with a very enterprising B.C., I think it was well ahead of the rest of us. B.C.'s vied with one another for pamphlets to decorate the walls, although I doubt whether anyone read them, but the A.R.P. people and the Ministry of Information produced numerous and sometimes humorous posters, many of which now adorned the training room. Models of enemy and friendly aircraft hung down from the ceiling, to assist in identification, and model ships and silhouettes to assist in ship recognition were often made by the battery members themselves. The regimental commander and indeed any other visitors to a battery invariably made a point of visiting the training room. The training programme had to be very carefully compiled with a variety of subjects, and then a copy forwarded to the R.H.Q. for approval. If, for instance, layers training or dummy loader appeared too often and for too long, a frigid comment would be received from the adjutant that the B.C. was doing little to hold the men's interest, and the programme would have to be revised. B.C.'s were continually searching their brains for new ideas. It was considered that 20 to 30 minutes was the maximum period for lecturing on any one subject and no lectures were allowed immediately after the mid-day meal, when it was felt that the powers of absorption were at their lowest.

On one occasion I was faced with an unforeseen difficulty. A party of about 12 Welsh lads were attached to the Eastern Arm battery on a temporary basis, for instruction on the twin six, before posting ·to another unit, shortly to be equipped with similar guns. A training programme was drawn up and approved by R.H.Q., who insisted that, on the completion of the course, a small written examination and test should be set to determine the amount of success achieved by the training officers and also to aid in the selection of future N.C.O.'s. The test paper

66

was approved by R.H.Q., who wanted a detailed list of marks. The questions were by no means difficult. Such questions as 'What are the duties of a gun look-out?' and 'What would be your duties as No. 2 if the alarm sounded and you were not on duty?' At the end of three weeks, the lads all settled down to take the test, and I was greatly confident in the result. We had all conscientiously worked hard, and they were quite an intelligent crowd and seemed eager to learn. The practical side went off without a hitch. Most could strip the breech, and many put up quite a good effort in laying the gun and even datuming the auto-sight. We then underwent the short written test. Imagine my horror, therefore, when the papers were handed in, to find that nearly half of them had been written in Welsh. Whilst these lads conversed in English, it would appear that they were far more at home in writing Welsh. One very bright lad, had even taking a step further, and written his answers in verse, and a very fine effort it was too. I felt inclined to send these papers to R.H.Q. for translation, and then foresaw all the complications which would, inevitably, result. However I finally solved the difficulty by making each man verbally relate his answers to me, and I copied them down in English, and then marked them. They all did exceedingly well, but after about four weeks they returned to somewhere in Wales and I never heard of them again.

We were provided with some aids in this instruction and training. After all we were not schoolmasters, and daily classes, and progress in training, etc. was somewhat new to us. H.M. Stationery Office printed a small booklet on the subject, entitled 'Notes for Instruction on the

Principles of Instruction'. It was a grand title and had the usual government phraseology and gift of making three words do, when one would have been quite sufficient. However it informed us that instruction is most effective when the will to learn is present, and when the recruit is interested in the work in hand. This seemed to me to be very wise philosophy, if not rather obvious. It went on to inform us that the object of the instructor was to seek out methods whereby he could seek out and stimulate interest. This we had been doing for months now, trying to stimulate interest in our training rooms. The only aids or poster likely to raise interest at this stage, was the exhibition of a few ladies, scantily clad, or the latest forces pin-up. This was not mentioned in the government book, but experience proved to us that it was the most effective. On the lantern on which we showed our slides, we occasionally slipped in a picture of an alluring blonde, and that always kept the

interest of the onlookers alive. This was not included in our manual of instruction, and whereas the principles set out in the instruction book could well apply in a holding battalion or training centre, they were not easy to apply in a small room at the end of a concrete mole, in winter, and by an officer who had probably been on watch all night.

The pupils were there, because they had been called up, and were ordered to be there, but at the back of their minds, no doubt, were such thoughts as the next guard duty they would be called upon to attend, or how to keep out of the biting wind or keep themselves dry from a running sea, splashing over the parapet on which they were standing.

But still in the winter months of the end of 1939 and the beginning of 1940, we managed. The temper and the spirit in the batteries were good. There was the odd time when an hour or so could be spent in the town, and the greater part of the battery personnel were still territorials, and

The winter months of 1939-40 on the Pier Turret Battery, during the phoney war.

known to one another, if not in civilian life, certainly in the drill halls. 159 from Brighton and Lewes had settled down in Newhaven and on the Southern Breakwater on their 6 inch guns; 170 from Ramsgate were now installed on the Pier Turret 6 inch and 12 pounders on the Pier Extension and at the end of the Ramsgate pier; Langdon had the remaining men from 159 and the Dover battery — 168 were manning Eastern Arm and Citadel. An effort was made to give some variation by inter-changing the batteries, but it was not very popular, as it tended to break up friendships and separate old buddies. The officers were changed about. I started off at the Citadel, then to Langdon, but in December, 1939, I was posted to Eastern Arm where I remained for the next seven or eight months.

The war seemed very remote. A stalemate existed on the Western front, and any attack on the port seemed a long way away. A large number of trawlers, now converted to minesweepers, were based at the port, the *Maretta* and *Fyldea* to name but a couple, and the crews, when not on duty, visited the canteens on the Pier Turret and Eastern Arm for a drink and a sing-song or a game of darts. The trawlers or minesweepers, as they were now called, had on board, in addition to the trawler skipper, a naval unit officer, usually a lieutenant of the R.N.V.R., no doubt to ensure that naval discipline was maintained, and provide the additional knowledge required for trawling mines instead of fish. The naval unit officer was not the captain of the ship and the command still remained in the hands of the original skipper. They were all an extremely friendly and cheerful crowd, although their job was a very hazardous one, and they certainly helped to relieve the monotony, which was developing after a few months of inactivity. Later on in the war, officers of the regiment, in their spare time, and with permission of the regimental commander, and naval authority, were permitted to go on short sea trips on the sweepers, when they made their daily sweep up and down the Strait to keep a channel clear of mines for the convoys. This had the double purpose of giving the officers concerned an insight into the workings of that part of the navy and also an opportunity of inspecting our defences from the sea, and give them additional ideas for camouflaging and means of defence. I was fortunate enough to make a number of these trips, sometimes without the necessary permission, but I was never found out.

On the Eastern Arm, we had another naval officer, a lieutenant permanently attached. He was the boom defence officer responsible for opening and closing the boom, on instructions from the P.W.S.S. The troops affectionately referred to him as 'Gertie Dogfish' and if he knew, he did not seem to mind, being always willing to join in a game of darts in the canteen or a sherry with me in our little concrete room. He had a similar quarter a little farther down the Arm, and we shared the one small lavatory at the end of the block. There was a rather delapidated hand-basin fitted, which, on pressing a knob, produced a strange coloured water, which could have been either sea water or sewage water. One thing it was not, and that was fresh water. However, this was our only washing facility, and during the very cold spell, when snow fell, it was a bit chilly going down the Arm to shave in the ice cold water.

On some Sundays we were visited by a padre, sent along by the senior chaplain in Dover. The local T.A. doctor, who previously had a practice in Dover, which he had abandoned when called up, would visit us occasionally for a drink and chat. He was concerned about our health and sleeping arrangements. Men were sleeping about ten to a compartment at least, but I assured him that they preferred it that way, as it helped to keep them warm. He was concerned about the amount of fine coal dust which seemed to seep in everywhere, even on the gun floor, from the large, now disused coal bunker, under which the barrack rooms were being built. In fact we did have a number of cases of impetigo, and he ordered that on every fine occasion, all blankets were to be hung out on lines to be erected across the Arm. It rather looked as if we were having a permanent wash day, and we suffered some derisive remarks from our naval friends. But somehow we managed. The doctor was fortunate, in as much as his wife was also a doctor, and was able to continue his practice, and attend his patients, during his absence in the army.

At a later date, a medical inspection room was set up in Langdon Barracks, on top of the cliffs. Anyone reporting sick and able to walk, was required not only to walk the length of the Arm, but also enter a tunnel cut into the base of the cliff. This long, steep, but illuminated tunnel, cut in the chalk, climbed up through the cliff and emerged eventually inside Langdon Barracks. It was, indeed, a long, tiring and tedious climb, and it is therefore not surprising how few we had reporting sick on the Eastern Arm. By the time they reached the medical inspection room in Langdon Barracks they were either perfectly fit again or dead. If they were neither, it indicated that they were shamming.

For the batteries on the western side of the harbour, Pier Turret and Pier Extension, a similar long walk was required by those reporting sick. They were required to attend the medical inspection room in Archcliffe Fort, although they did not have to climb the cliff to reach their destination. South Breakwater, marooned on the central jetty could only come ashore by launch, to the Prince of Wales Pier, usually ferried by an ancient craft, known as the *Seymour Castle*. Before the war, this old boat used to run pleasure trips from Dover to Dungeness, but how she stayed afloat so long was a mystery. She finally disappeared, but it was interesting to note that a year or so later, when I was joining a troopship at Greenock in Scotland, who should ferry me out but the old *Seymour Castle*. Whether this was her final resting place, I do not know. It only amazed me at the time that she had managed to get from Dover to Scotland without being sunk either by the enemy or through natural causes.

Excepting Langdon Battery therefore, no man was encouraged to report sick from any of the harbour batteries. Citadel Battery had its own M.I. room inside the Citadel complex, where it was used by a number of infantry and anti-aircraft personnel.

The barracks at Langdon were originally an old convict prison and part of it was built by French prisoners of war during the Napoleonic

Opposite
*Quarters on the
Western Head of the
Southern Breakwater.*

70

wars. It had a very high wall surrounding the whole perimeter, and part of this wall still remained standing, whilst piles of bricks bore evidence where the remaining wall had once stood. The main prison buildings had been built on two levels, in steps of about 30 feet, but these buildings had long since disappeared and both site levels cleared. There were, however, a number of buildings on the slopes at the perimeter, which had no doubt once been the prison laundry, store rooms, etc. and a large arched gateway provided the entrance to the roadway. A guard was provided at this entrance. These rooms now provided excellent store rooms for the regimental quartermasters and district officers who were now housed there. The ration store and skidding, which was in fact, large blocks of wood, ropes, blocks and tackle, used for gun shifting and barrel changing, were also housed in these buildings and of course our friend, the M.I. room. There was no armament or air defence within the barrack compound, and the defence came within the scope of Langdon Battery, situated at the top eastern end of the barracks, but outside the perimeter. From these levels on the high cliffs, one had a long uninterrupted view across the Channel and on a clear day, the cliffs of France at Cap Blanc Nez and Cap Griz Nez can be clearly seen. Even the tall tower of Calais Hotel de Ville can be seen through binoculars. Today whilst the buildings have now all gone, and the gateway demolished, many visitors park their cars on these levels, unaware of the history surrounding them, and they enjoy the view of the Eastern Dock, with all its hovercraft and ferry activity. The gateway has gone, and where the guard was mounted, there is now an ice cream kiosk!

Let us however return to the days of 1939/40. I have endeavoured to give the reader some idea of the general set-up of the regiment and the defences of Dover until May, 1940, when the storm broke and the whole aspect changed. Dover then became very much in the front line and its defences and organisation became of paramount importance.

8 The storm breaks

Of all the trees that grow so fair,
   Old England to adorn,
Greater are none beneath the sun
   Than the Oak and Ash and Thorn.

Sing Oak and Ash and Thorn, good sirs,
   (All of a midsummer morn)
Surely we sing no little thing,
   In Oak and Ash and Thorn.

Sink Oak and Ash and Thorn, good sirs,
   (All of a midsummer morn)
England shall bide till Judgment tide,
   By Oak and Ash and Thorn.

              Rudyard Kipling. *A Tree Song* (A.D. 1200)

We were first alerted of impending disaster, not only by the press but also the considerable number of ships entering the port, laden with troops. They certainly did not give the appearance of troops returning on furlough. But a few days later in May, the armada of ships, little ships, big ships, destroyers, trawlers, motor boats, life boats and in fact anything that floated left the port on its memorable journey to the Dunkirk beaches. From the cliffs and even from the harbour moles, we could see a bright glow in the sky where Calais burned. This time, not from the hands of the English as so often had happened in the past, but from the hands of the Germans, and English soldiers, together with their allies the French, were endeavouring to defend the town. This could not have happened many times in history. Later we could see where Dunkirk itself and Boulogne were in flames. Very soon boats of all sizes and description appeared before the harbour. Besides many of the vessels which had left a few hours earlier, there were now rowing boats, yachts, and even a raft, on which sat a large Frenchman, clutching a pig.

Obviously the examination service and battery could do little against such a vast array of ships. It was impossible to fire 'bring to' rounds, without hitting some other vessel, besides which many were in distress

Above
Allied soldiers finding refuge in Britain after fleeing from the Dunkirk beaches.
Right
Another boat loaded with British soldiers arrives back in Dover from France.

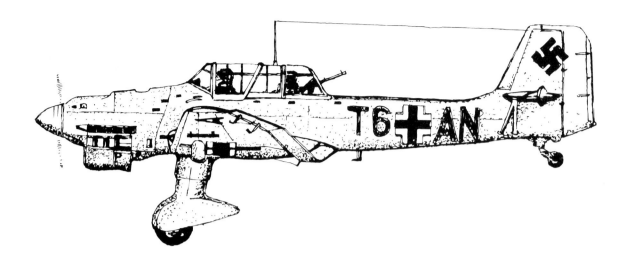

and carried wounded aboard, so it was essential that they entered the harbour as quickly as possible. The naval authorities were quite adamant, however, and stated quite clearly that no vessel was to enter the port until it had been passed by the examination service. They supplemented the service by adding a vessel of their own, to assist the examination vessel, who was frantically steaming from one vessel to another. We later heard that she had been run down in the night by a larger vessel and sunk but it was not surprising in view of the congestion in the waters outside the Eastern Entrance. The navy were aware that the opportunity now presented itself for undesirable agents and fifth columnists to enter the country, and saboteurs had a fine chance with anything which took their fancy, with little chance of being caught, in the general confusion now prevailing. At one time, I counted no less than 140 vessels outside the port and the examination vessel could do little more than signal the P.W.S.S., who in turn advised the Eastern Arm Battery. If there had been a concerted rush for the entrance, there would have been little we could have done to stop them. Many of the vessels had not the facility and in some cases, even the masts, to fly any recognition signal, so they could only be indentified by sign and description. It was not practicable to keep opening and closing the boom, so it remained open all the time. If a vessel had made a dash for the entrance, and many did so, neither Langdon nor Eastern Arm could fire preventative shots. The problem was finally partially solved by the duty officer on Eastern Arm, who maintained an open line direct to the fire commander and hence the P.W.S.S. He sat on top of the concrete parapet, above the harbour entrance, armed with a .303 rifle which he fired as near as possible to the bows of an offending vessel, not always with success. If one entered illegally, he could only advise the P.W.S.S., who arranged for the vessel to be boarded inside the harbour or alongside the jetty.

Many of the vessels approaching were French. The wretched duty officer, not knowing the French for 'examination vessel' and in fact, knowing very little French at all, could only shout through a megaphone 'Arrête . . . . Approchez-vous la Raisonère'. Sometimes it worked, but

The Junkers Ju 87 Stuka dive bomber. Its whine, as it dived, was designed to strike fear into the enemy.

more often it did not, and it was unlikely he would have been understood, even if he had been heard. Obviously if it was observed that a vessel had injured men on board, or was in need of urgent medical attention, or was in danger of sinking, she was given priority, and no effort was made to impede her entrance into the harbour.

The sea was absolutely flat calm and the weather fine and clear. If the enemy had had the resources, or ability, to bring over his JU 87's or ME 109's, a perfect sitting target presented itself, and considerable loss of life and damage would undoubtedly have resulted. We have much to thank the R.A.F. for not allowing him to do so.

The tragedy of Dunkirk is well known and has been related many times. It suffices to record that the main bulk of the army returned in small boats, many so gallantly manned by both amateur and professional sailors; there is no question that this feat in itself was magnificent, but nevertheless, it was a defeat. The British army had been driven from the continent, losing the major part of its weapons and equipment. Many of our friends lay dead or captured. The local infantry battalion, The Buffs, Territorial Army, our friends from the neighbouring drill hall, had been decimated, and it was very difficult to understand that we should not see them again. They were all local lads, and we knew them all well. We competed against them in the Emden Trophy, before the war, and many worked in the same offices and factories as ourselves. It seemed unbelievable that most of them had now gone. Dunkirk was certainly no victory, only the gallant men who had fought the rearguard actions and defended Calais, had made the rescue of the army possible. The R.A.F. had played their part, and the navy had thrown in everything, with considerable loss in ships and men.

Vessels of all shapes and sizes tied up alongside the Eastern Arm, Admiralty Pier and Prince of Wales Pier, at whatever berths they could find. There are many stories of spirit and morale. Morale was high because so many were relieved to be home again and out of the hell they had so recently survived. A few units marched ashore and fell in with the same discipline as a Guards Regiment. Their uniforms may not have looked as if they were going on parade, many were wounded, and nearly exhausted, but their fall-in and march off was impeccable, and an example to many, and filled one with a sense of pride. Alas some other units or bodies of men, for it had been almost impossible to keep them in their battalions and regiments during the scramble to get aboard, were not so disciplined. Morale in many cases was extremely low, even to the extent of throwing away valuable and much needed arms and weapons into the sea, a sight which I regret was not too uncommon.

Morale on the Eastern Arm itself was not helped by the stacking of bodies, some badly mutilated, just outside the battery perimeter. One unfortunate officer, not of my regiment, informed me that it was his duty, and a very distressing one, to endeavour to recover the identity discs from each body, in order to list the names of the casualties.

Vessels were now moored alongside the Arm in very battered conditions, and many of the naval ships were displaying two White Ensigns, to indicate that they had recently been in action. In many cases there was only an improvised pole on which to fly them. The mast and often the bridge itself demolished or battered out of all recognition.

We set up trestle tables along the Arm and an obliging publican in Dover let us have a number of barrels of beer. When we sent a 15 cwt. truck to his pub and explained why we were in such a hurry he let us have all he had, and even returned with us, to give us a hand. Some of his customers must have gone short for a few days. We were determined that any man coming ashore, should have a glass of beer if he wanted it. We had insufficient glasses, so all the troops lent their mugs. Instructions were given that no charge was to be made, but the navy came along afterwards and asked to be allowed to reimburse us with the cost and we reached some compromise. They also sent us a very nice letter.

I met a seaman on the mole, who at first sight appeared to be badly wounded. He seemed to be covered in blood and even his boots were squelching. I pulled him into our little mess, thinking I could render him some first aid, until the ambulance arrived, but to my surprise, he assured me that he was quite uninjured — he had just brought his skipper, or what was left of him, ashore in a sack. They had apparently been about to enter Boulogne Harbour, and all had seemed moderately quiet. Suddenly, he informed me, a devasting fire had been opened on the ship from a very short range. They had no idea the port was in German hands, and had sailed into a trap. The officers were all killed or wounded and the ship almost turned into a wreck. However, by going hard astern, she had escaped and a leading seaman had navigated her home.

There were many and varied tales to tell of those last days, before the French channel ports fell, and many deeds of heroism went unnoticed. Destroyers were reported to be firing their torpedoes up the sand dunes, in a desperate effort to assist the army and harass the enemy, and some vessels returning home were so shot to pieces that it was a miracle they stayed afloat. One vessel, a small merchantman in peacetime, named *Killarney*, tied up alongside the Arm and within the battery perimeter. She had been hit by a large shell on her deckhouse, which at the time had been crowded with men, picked up from the beaches. The carnage is impossible to describe, as the occupants were literally blown to pieces, and the vessel resembled a slaughterhouse.

Another rather pathetic scene to which we were party, was the arrival of a young French doctor aboard a small French fishing vessel. He had been to Paris on a visit and was returning by train, so he told us, to his family who lived in Boulogne. The train had been halted a mile or so outside Boulogne by what appeared to be army tanks across the line. They turned out to be, to everybody's amazement and alarm, German tanks. Nobody had anticipated the enemy was so close and it seemed

impossible that they were so far into France, and not then even under attack. No warning had been given to the Railway Company that there was any likelihood of possible danger or that the line to the coast would even be under attack. It was quite probable that the headquarters of the railway had no idea either. The train occupants were all ordered to leave the train, but what happened to them, our doctor friend did not know. Somehow he managed to conceal himself in the embankment and his presence went unnoticed by the captors. He endeavoured to make his way by foot to Boulogne, anxious about his family, but found his way blocked by parties of German troops and tanks. There appeared to be fighting in the streets of Boulogne and the town in flames. Only a few days earlier, he had left it in peace and going about its normal business and trade. He managed to reach the coast well to the east of the town, and made his way down to the beach. He was fortunate enough to be sighted by the small French fishing vessels, who had been returning to their home port after fishing, and had been fired upon as they approached the harbour. They were as bewildered as the doctor. They had suffered no damage, and having put to sea again, were wondering where they should sail to now. They had sighted the doctor waving frantically from the shore, and had decided to pick him up. There seemed little else for them to do, but to make for Dover harbour, so in this respect the doctor was at least fortunate in not being recaptured. He had lunch with us but naturally he was very distressed and worried about the fate of his family, as were the crews of the two fishing vessels.

Late that afternoon, on the advice of the naval authorities they were instructed to put to sea and make for the port of Le Havre. We never saw them again, and I wondered what happened to them and whether they were ever united with their families.

Looking back on the devastated beaches of northern France.

77

Another vessel came alongside the Arm, carrying a number of Senegalese troops, some of whom had been badly wounded. We rendered what aid we could, until the arrival of the naval ambulances, but one poor fellow actually died in my arms. I put a cigarette in his mouth and I suppose by way of thanks, he gave me his steel helmet, but died almost immediately afterwards.

We also had a number of nurses arrive late one night, at least thirty in all, who had been bombed out at the British base hospital in Boulogne. Their matron had been killed, but nevertheless they were in very good spirit considering all the hardships and danger they had obviously undergone. It was about 1 a.m. and we made them some hot tea in the canteen. One whispered to me that they would like to spend a penny, and the only suitable place I could think of was our little concrete lavatory at the end of the battery. They therefore formed a chain and with myself leading, with a small torch, we made our way down the Arm. On reflection, we must have been rather a curious spectacle. They were later picked up by the naval authorities, and taken back to the naval headquarters in the town, where no doubt they found more comfortable facilities. I was deeply impressed by these dedicated and cheerful women, who had obviously done so much to lift the morale of the troops, as well as providing a skilful and humane service in very difficult and trying conditions.

Before concluding this brief report of the arrival back of some of the troops from the beaches of Dunkirk, as seen through the eyes of the men on the Eastern Arm, I should like to put on record one further and extremely valuable service rendered by the Royal Navy. It concerns *H.M.S. Sabre.* She was a small type of destroyer, some 900 tons displacement and completed at the end of the First World War. The skipper and I became quite friendly, and he shared with me our concern over the lack of armament and ammunition, and the amount being left on the beaches and on the quayside by the evacuating army. He promised me, therefore, that on each trip he made, he would endeavour to lay hands on any abandoned equipment and ammunition, whatever it happened to be. He was as good as his word, for in all he provided me with no less than nine Bren guns, and a number of boxes of ammunition. On his last trip, he even provided me with a Boys anti-tank rifle, but could only find seventeen rounds of ammunition for it. This was the final gift, and it was a miracle that he even survived this last journey. The ship's funnel looked like a pepperpot, and the bridge and deck a mass of twisted metal. There were many deeds of bravery and heroism during those fateful weeks that will forever go unsung and unrecorded. It seemed that men would go to any length of endurance with complete disregard for personal safety, once their homeland was threatened, or their honour at stake. We were indeed fortunate to find such men during one of the most critical times in our history.

Some of the guns given to me were encrusted with sand from the Dunkirk beaches, but it was not long before we had these cleaned up and put into serviceable condition. Hastily we built new strong points, with sandbags filled with chalk, which we had in abundance. These strong

The Boys Mark 1 anti-tank rifle. With a calibre of 13·97mm it had an armour penetration of 21mm at 300 metres. The gun had an overall length of 1·6 metres.

points were sited to prevent an attack on the battery itself, in the event of a full scale invasion, for without the use of these newly acquired Bren guns, it had not been possible to provide such protection. The Boys anti-tank rifle was particularly useful. We sited it on the parapet in front of No. 1 gun, and facing across the eastern entrance. It would certainly make a hole in the side of any motor boat or even landing craft, and we reckoned that an E-boat attempting to force the entrance could well be crippled by our newly acquired weapon. We trained a couple of men to man it, and they were instructed always to aim at the waterline, which we reckoned would probably be most effective. It did, however, have a kick like a mule, but as we could only spare one round for practice and there was no possible chance of any replacement, only one person got a bruised shoulder. The army is rather peculiar about any unit having equipment or men for that matter, which it refers to as 'surplus to establishment.' If it had become generally known that I had acquired these additional weapons, notwithstanding the circumstances by which they were obtained, or the fact that they might play a vital role in the defence of the port and possibly the country, I should have been required to surrender them to the proper authorities, and possibly received some rebuke for being so impertinent as to imagine that I could equip myself with weapons beyond those laid down in the establishment manual. The Corps Commander Coast Artillery was well aware of their existence, and I know he wished me well, because when visiting the battery on one occasion, he told me to tell him when to close his eyes, so that he should not see anything he was not meant to see.

There was another instance worth recording. This did little to raise my morale. It had now become obvious that the British Army or what was left of it as a fighting force, had now been evacuated from the continent, and most of its equipment had been abandoned or lost. Until the army could be regrouped and its equipment replaced, it was not going to be in a position to offer organised resistance to an enemy, flushed with victory, who invaded our shores in the immediate future. A large ship arrived in Dover harbour and tied up alongside the Eastern Arm. She was the *S.S. Mona's Isle*, formerly a ferry, I believe, operating between the Isle of Man and the mainland. She was loaded with anti-tank and anti-

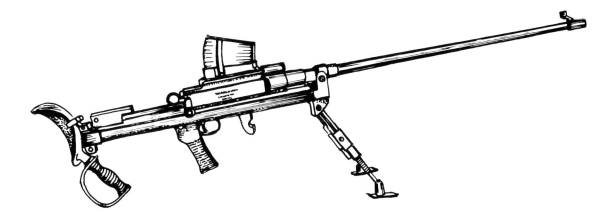

personnel mines, as well as other explosives, and her destination had been Dunkirk, which was now in enemy hands. It caused some alarm in the battery. If she had been hit by an enemy bomb, such would be the explosion, that our battery would stand little chance of survival, and other ships moored nearby would be severely damaged. The skipper was urged to move away but no doubt had his orders to berth alongside us and was not going to move. He came and sat with me all one night, whilst I was on watch, inside our B.O.P., but indeed proved to be very much a Job's Comforter. He informed me that in his opinion, we would be invaded within the next 72 hours, at most, and probably sooner. He could see no means of stopping the invincible German army, and that we, on the Eastern Arm, would have to take the first onslaught. He felt very sorry for us, and was convinced that within the next week, we should all be dead. And so we were glad when, shortly afterwards, he received orders to move to some other safer location, and I never saw his ship again.

Very soon, orders were received by all batteries to make themselves secure both from land and sea attack. In the case of Southern Breakwater, this presented no great problem, whilst Citadel and Langdon were faced with quite a mammoth task. We had never reckoned on being attacked from the rear. I was already engaged in building my strong points and arming them with my newly acquired weapons, and both the Turret Battery and ourselves were concerned with blocking off any approach along the piers. We did place chalk bags along the parapets, to save bullets ricocheting off the concrete, and we also erected a small barbed wire barrier by the guard room, covered by a strong point and a Bren gun. It was here that I had the idea of driving iron stakes into the concrete, about six inches high, and attaching to them, single strands of barbed wire in a cross-cross pattern across the Arm. I thought that if we were attacked at night, a superior force rushing along the Arm would be tripped up and put into some confusion. The weakness lay in the fact that we had to leave a sufficient gap to allow the passage of a motor vehicle. It also put us into confusion sometimes, when we forgot that they were there, and as they were never tried out, I shall never know whether they would have worked. In any case, they and us would probably have been neutralised by our own heavy batteries, situated at Shepherdswell, some few miles behind the town. In the case of Langdon and Citadel, it meant erecting massive barbed wire defences, which were later protected by minefields and concrete strong points.

One final defence was given to the Eastern Arm and Pier Extension, to operate in an emergency. This was three 21 inch torpedo tubes, erected on fixed mountings, and sited across the harbour entrances. They were to be fired, only at point blank range, when the German troopships were entering the harbour. Initially they were the navy responsibility, but, in an emergency, we were to be instructed on how to fire them, always providing we were still in a position to do so.

When our ammunition had been expended, and the guns were of no further use, we were instructed to remove parts of the breech on each equipment. It was essential that the same parts on each gun be removed, so that the enemy could not cannibalise one gun, in order to put the other in action. The parts to be removed, were to be thrown into the sea.

The final orders were to the effect that whatever happened, we would be expected to stop the first three waves of the invading forces. It was essential that we did so, in order to provide the time for the Royal Navy to arrive in some strength, and they would then throw everything they had into the forces of the invading army. The time factor was essential. Whatever happened, the enemy must not be allowed to establish a bridgehead or form a valuable base in Dover, or even gain advantage from any of the port's facilities. If the enemy managed to land on the Arm, our orders were to counter-attack immediately. This would possibly have presented some difficulty, especially if we were still in a position to service the guns. The higher authorities may possibly have overlooked the fact that our total strength, without casualties, and including the cooks, was 2 officers and 70 men. This seemed to provide an adequate reason why we should see to it that the enemy did not gain a foothold, and must be destroyed at sea. I was even asked to submit my plan of counter-attack, should the enemy breach our perimeter and even at the time, it did seem rather farcical. At best, our combined forces for counter-attack could not have exceeded one officer and ten men, these being mainly non-operational personnel. It would appear that the higher command were clutching at straws, and I often wonder exactly what would have happened if the Germans had been in a position to launch a full scale invasion attack in those early days. There is no doubt that they would have had their problems, with lack of proper and adequate shipping, lack of invasion training by their troops, and certainly not full command of the air space above. The result can only be a guess. There is no doubt, however, that the fighting would have been extremely fierce and bloody, and even in these conditions, luck itself would play quite a part. Luck whether we hit the right ships at the right time, luck on the weather conditions, luck on the speed that support could arrive, and by the enemy on gaining a sufficient surprise. As far as morale was concerned, the troops were supremely confident that they could stop anything, and I heard the remark that they wished the enermy would try. One big failure now by the enemy, they thought would bring a rapid conclusion to the war. I wonder!

Thus the Dunkirk episode closed. We had come through a phase which had, in a short period, turned us from Saturday afternoon soldiers into what I hoped I could now consider an efficient fighting unit. We were by no means perfect, but we had sufficient training and experience to give a good account of ourselves. The batteries of Southern Breakwater, Admiralty Pier, Langdon and Citadel were very much of the same feeling as the troops on the Arm. We now boasted that we were the nearest fighting troops to the enemy and Britain's front line. This was in fact quite true.

The type of attack that could be expected would be: —
(1)   A lightning attack on the port by destroyers.
(2)   A more concentrated attack by E-boats and S-boats.

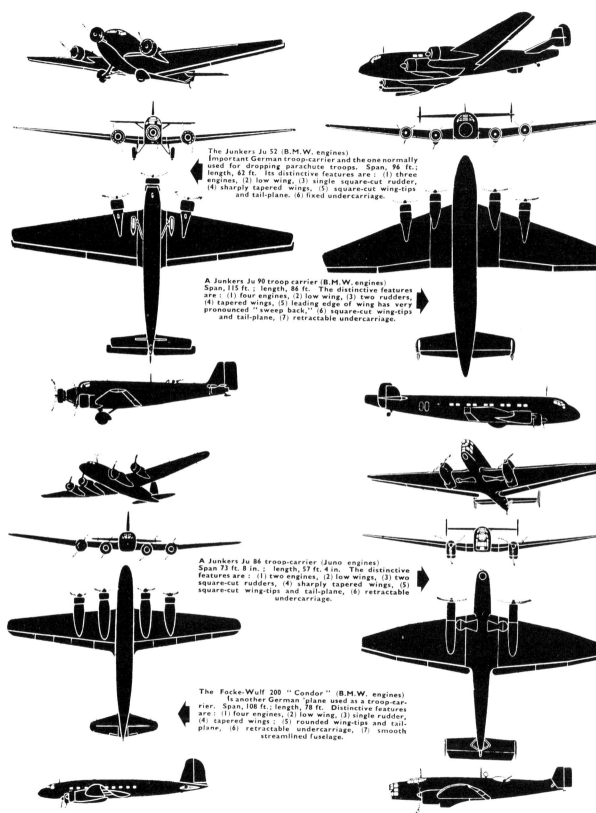

The Junkers Ju 52 (B.M.W. engines)
Important German troop-carrier and the one normally used for dropping parachute troops. Span, 96 ft.; length, 62 ft. Its distinctive features are : (1) three engines, (2) low wing, (3) single square-cut rudder, (4) sharply tapered wings, (5) square-cut wing-tips and tail-plane. (6) fixed undercarriage.

A Junkers Ju 90 troop carrier (B.M.W. engines)
Span, 115 ft. ; length, 86 ft. The distinctive features are : (1) four engines, (2) low wing, (3) two rudders, (4) tapered wings, (5) leading edge of wing has very pronounced "sweep back," (6) square-cut wing-tips and tail-plane, (7) retractable undercarriage.

A Junkers Ju 86 troop-carrier (Juno engines)
Span 73 ft. 8 in. ; length, 57 ft. 4 in. The distinctive features are : (1) two engines, (2) low wings, (3) two square-cut rudders, (4) sharply tapered wings, (5) square-cut wing-tips and tail-plane, (6) retractable undercarriage.

The Focke-Wulf 200 "Condor" (B.M.W. engines)
Is another German 'plane used as a troop-carrier. Span, 108 ft.; length, 78 ft. Distinctive features are : (1) four engines, (2) low wing, (3) single rudder, (4) tapered wings ; (5) rounded wing-tips and tail-plane, (6) retractable undercarriage, (7) smooth streamlined fuselage.

(3)   Attack by a boomsmasher, possibly disguised as a merchantman, but preparing the way for a more concentrated attack.

(4)   Commando type raids by sea or by parachute, to destroy port installations, coast batteries, and to hold part of the coast, even for a few hours for propaganda purposes. It was felt that if any part of Dover could be captured by the enemy, and held for a few hours, it would give a tremendous boost to the German propaganda machine in the eyes of the rest of the world.

Any of these types of attack could be the prelude to full scale invasion, and a combination of two of the attacks must be very much more probable.

It was only a short distance by sea to cross, and an attack by enemy capital ships was considered very improbable. But we had to be prepared for the most unlikely and unexpected assault on the most unanticipated target. The enemy was bound to make some probing move, before launching a full scale invasion, and committing all his forces.

It must be borne in mind that, at this stage, no early warning could be relied upon from radio location sources. The A.A. detection was rapidly being developed, and the towers constructed behind Langdon could not be adapted to give warning of a sea attack. Two sets of M1 and M2, were almost ready, but they were in an experimental stage, and their reliability was somewhat in question at this time. They could not be used for rangefinders for the guns.

In the main, therefore, the primary source of warning fell to the gun look-outs themselves. Their alertness was now of paramount importance. Considerable training and effort was accordingly applied to these duties. Men were trained to become 'dark accustomed.' Gun reliefs were never changed until the new relief had satisfied himself that his eyes were converted from the lighted war shelter, to the dark sea in front of him. Ranges were constructed with model ships in darkened rooms, and training was carried out to accustom men to recognise the shape and direction of ships in the very gloomiest conditions. Night glasses were provided for all look-outs and it was a very serious offence if any man was found either asleep or not concentrating on the sea area in front of him. A look-out was posted to each gun, and these look-outs were never changed at the same time, so to ensure that at least one was used to the dark, and the period of look-out never exceeded one hour. The 6 inch had fighting lights and it was stressed that they should be exposed, on the very slightest suspicion. When a light was exposed, a report was immediately phoned to the fire commander, giving the reason, but it was always encouraged to expose, if any doubt whatsoever existed.

The illuminated areas in front of the eastern and western entrances, according to weather conditions, would only give a maximum range of 1200 yards in the best conditions. Accordingly a fast moving motor boat approaching the harbour would require very little time, and it must be engaged by the batteries before it came too close and so out of the range, as the guns could not be depressed below a fixed angle. It was essential, therefore, that the gun detachments were housed as near their equipment as possible, and they were trained, night after night, to take

With the possibility of air-borne invasion the War Office issued leaflets showing the silhouettes of German troop-carrying aeroplanes.

83

post with the greatest possible speed, and the officer on watch to engage the target without the slightest hesitation. There was certainly no time for hesitation or verification. The detachments practised away and regrettably there were often many curses in the dark, and some sprained or broken ankles. They were expected to rush out of the lighted gun shelters, immediately the alarm bell rang, leap across the parapet, and take up their gun positions. It was a small wonder that we never lost anybody over the side. It was practised every night with monotonous regularity, and in spite of a few accidents, gradually the time improved, until on the Eastern Arm, we reckoned we could get the first round off within 6 seconds of the alarm ringing. Even this was too long in reality, but before the introduction of some form of early warning radar, it was the best we could do in early June, 1940, short of manning the guns all night on the gunfloor itself. This must inevitably have led to inefficiency, as it was quite unreasonable to suppose that the detachments could stand round the guns all night.

The C.A. S. L. engines were kept running all night, and the lights exposed behind closed shutters, to ensure that the illuminated area could be put into operation within a second or two. A false alarm was by no means frowned upon, and indeed, was sometimes a welcome break to the long monotony of the night. The exposure of light, and temporary break in blackout restrictions, did not appear to encourage any enemy aircraft, and I do not recall the exposure of the searchlights being followed by an air attack. The greatest problem was to keep the detachments alert and awake in the war shelters. A change-over of watches was sometimes arranged at 0200 hours, to ensure that both detachments got some sleep, but it was a punishable offence to fall asleep in the war shelter. Dart boards, cards, books, etc. were provided, and wireless could be played, provided it was not heard outside the shelter and in any way impeded the gun look-out's vigilance. No equipment or clothing could be removed

Searchlight positions, looking out to sea, one with the shutters open.

inside the shelter, and rifles were kept neatly stacked in racks. On rare occasions, when the weather was particularly bad, and the detachments were constantly being soaked by the sea breaking over the moles and breakwater, the corps commander, on the recommendation of the medical officer, would authorise a rum issue. Each battery held jars of S.R.D. rum, usually stored away in the B.C.'s office under lock and key as well as being sealed. When an issue was authorised, the B.C. accompanied by the B.S.M. would visit every man, who was obliged to consume his ration in the presence of the B.C. They were allowed to have it poured into a mug of tea. Unless one witnessed the drinking, some of the older sweats would bargain or entice the younger members of the battery to part with their ration. There was, however, one tradition which was carefully followed. An additional ration was given to the man on watch who could throw a dart nearest to the 'bull'. The issued rum was accountable, and involved certificates and returns, etc.

The men seemed to realise their responsibilities, and the seriousness of the situation, for we had very little trouble indeed. The position was accepted, and somehow, the gun No. 1's kept their detachments together and on their toes. During the winter nights, especially when it was bitterly cold, it was difficult to remain vigilant, and even more so, if you had rain and sleet and snow, in addition to the occasional wave, beating into your face, and your hands were frozen to the marrow. But the fear was always there. He might attack at any time of day, and certainly when we least expected him to. It became less likely after September had passed, but we dared not take any chances. It is interesting to note, that when the weather was particularly cold, and temperatures were down to zero and below, concern was felt for the six inch guns becoming frozen. Instructions were received for a brick to be heated up and placed inside the barrel at the breech end. This would ensure that the obturation pad on the B.L. guns did not freeze up, and so make them unserviceable. If they had gone into action suddenly, and the presence of the brick had been overlooked, I cannot imagine what would have happened. It certainly might have conveyed to the enemy that we were short of ammunition!

It was not long after the Dunkirk evacuation that the enemy began to make his presence known. He did so, by continuous air attacks on the harbour installations, ships in the harbour and on the harbour batteries. He made no attempt at this stage to bomb the town of Dover itself. The batteries were frequently machine-gunned, and the enemy became almost regular in his habits, certainly as far as the Eastern Arm was concerned, as low flying machine-gun attacks, the length of the Arm, usually took place at 8 a.m. daily. From the large number of Bren guns I had been able to obtain from *H.M.S. Sabre*, I selected one, and for no reason whatsoever, named it 'Stella'. It was just a name that occurred to me, as I knew of nobody by that name. Stella, together with two or three loaded magazines, was kept in our small mess and sleeping quarters, and, on occasions, battery office. It was all the same room, until the wooden hut was completed for us on top of the mole. When these machine-gun attacks took place, it was up to the officer off watch to poke

Stella out of the door and have a go at them. It gave considerable satisfaction, if one was behind a gun and actually firing at the enemy, and far less frightening. Stella gave one a feeling of security, and although these actions, almost daily, lasted only a matter of seconds, they could be quite unpleasant if one was caught out in the open or just standing in a doorway, whilst pieces or chips of concrete flew in all directions from the machine-gun bullets. But with Stella it was different; one could at least hit back and gave one a great feeling of satisfaction, and no sense of fear existed. The enemy never seemed to drop any bombs at this stage, and was content to machine-gun. He did very little damage indeed, and some batteries did suffer a few casualties. I cannot in all honesty claim, however, that at any time was an enemy plane seriously damaged, let alone brought down, as a result of Stella's efforts, and I doubt whether the enemy pilot was ever aware of her existence, but it did our morale good, and so served its purpose. Of course there was another use for Stella, for in the event of an attack by sea or land, the off duty officer had at least one useful weapon at his disposal, and was far better off than the old 4.5 Colt revolvers with which we had been issued. We only had a limited amount of ammunition for these Colts, but when one fired the thing in practice, not only did it nearly break your wrist, but no degree of accuracy could be assured, so it was really much more danger to one's friends than to the enemy, if it came to close fighting. With Stella it was different, she would have been quite devastating, on small bunches of men rushing up the Arm.

One piece of air defence provided, I know not by whom, or who indeed manned them, consisted of a rectangular box. Two were fixed at the end of the Camber, at the entrance to the old submarine basin, now a haven for the motor torpedo boats. These weapons were known as unrifled projectiles or U.P.'s. They fired a group of projectiles all at the same time, and about twenty-four in number. Each projectile contained a small bomb, with a delayed action fuse of about 80 seconds and, when fired, a parachute opened out enabling the bomb to float through the air until it exploded. In order to make it more effective, beneath the bomb were suspended long lengths of wire. The theory was that if these projectiles could be fired in the path of attacking aircraft the wire would entangle in the plane's fuselage, and the bomb go off after a short while, so causing a 'kill'. The theory was certainly alright and they worked in as much as they went off according to plan. However, in practice, they always seem to be fired after the departure of the enemy and then drift across the harbour, a menace to the defenders themselves. The first time they fired, we had received no warning, and suddenly we were aware of a vast collection of parachutes, apparently over Langdon Battery. At a distance they resembled a parachute attack by the enemy. It was only when the bombs themselves started to explode, that we realised they were 'friendly'. I only recall seeing one of them actually bring down a plane, although there might have been others I had not witnessed. At the time the attack seemed to be conducted by Italian planes. One plane got the wire entangled in his tail, the bomb went off, completely blew off the rear of the plane and he nosed dived into the sea, right off the eastern entrance. We did not see the pilot escape and in fact the whole plane seemed to disappear beneath the sea in a matter of moments. Sometimes, however, the bombs did not go off. On one occasion, after an attack, one drifted slowly down on to the Arm with all its wire trailing behind it. The bomb seemed to lodge itself right outside our magazine door, where it hung suspended by an entanglement of wire. The B.S.M. and myself, equipped with wire cutters and with much trepidation, slowly freed it, and hurled it into the sea, where it sank without exploding. I reported the incident to the fire commander, who no doubt passed it on to the correct authorities. Shortly afterwards, I was requested to report why I had thrown it into the sea, and had not retained it, so that the bomb could be examined to find out why it had not gone off. My reply to this request was unprintable. It seems strange that in war time, some so-called experts have complete disregard for human life, and are only concerned if some of their apparatus fails to function.

On the subject of fear, I have often reflected what my feelings were or would have been, in the event of a prolonged attack, and possibly hand-to-hand fighting, or for that matter, constant shelling. It is true that a little later we were shelled sometimes without cessation for several days, and by a shell with a far larger calibre than anything we could then produce. The Junkers 87 dive bombers also had a number of goes at us so I could, in some measure, work out what my reactions were, after the event. To say that one was not frightened would be completely untrue, but I realised soon that it was something more than fear of being hit, it was fear of showing fear. I think I used to worry quite a lot that I would show fear in front of the men. The fact that I was really frightened did not seem to matter. One had to assume a mantle of rather stupid bravado, simply because one had a couple of pips on one's shoulder, and somehow convey this nonchalant air to the men, even if it was difficult to conceal that one's own knees were knocking. I was convinced, probably quite wrongly, that if ever I broke down, or let fear show itself in any way whatsoever, it would rapidly spread to the troops and panic and chaos would result. This theory is probably not true and no doubt somebody would have emerged to take command, but as far as I was concerned, it was the fear of being afraid, and showing it, that far out-weighed any other consideration.

I was later to see that panic spreads rapidly and can be contagious. I was on the gun floor of the twin six pounder, which had recently been erected on the Southern Breakwater, during a particularly long and vicious air attack. The electric cables had been damaged and operated the alarm, so we had taken post. As the tower had not been built, I positioned myself behind the gun. A member of the detachment suddenly started to shake and then scream, shouting that he intended to throw himself over the side. Within seconds the whole detachment started getting jumpy, and I was certain that unless I acted quickly, they would all take to their heels and seek the comparative safety of the war shelter, and no shouting from me would stop them. I did the only thing open to me and hit the gunner hard and practically knocked him out. It certainly stunned him, because he stopped shouting. The No. 1 and another member of the detachment grabbed him and took him below, and locked him up in a latrine for his own safety, until the action was over and we could attend to him for shock. This was an example of the rapid spread of panic, and I thought that perhaps it could have been me. The young man was in no way to blame. It was quite probable that only a few months earlier, like many others, he had been doing a quiet job in civvy street, and this was the first time he had witnessed the roar of the war. All hell had been let loose around us, and I was just as petrified as he was, but fighting not to show it. He was later transferred to another battery ashore, just in case he went over the side at a later date, and certainly no further action was taken in the matter.

We were no longer just another coast regiment, but with the appointment of our commanding officer, a Territorial and a former Dover College boy, to the rank of Brigadier, Corps Commander, Coast Artillery, we became corps troops, in 12 Corps, although the regiment still retained its name. The corps commander of 12th Corps was no less a person than General Bernard Montgomery. The three trees, the oak, the ash and the thorn were adopted as the emblem or corps sign and this we now wore on the sleeve of our uniforms. I understand that the sign was selected to link the name of the first corps commander, Sir A. F. Thorne, with the three trees, the oak, the ash and the thorn mentioned in Sir Rudyard Kipling's book *Puck of Pook's Hill*. It was the coastline covered by 12th Corps which was Pook's Hill country.

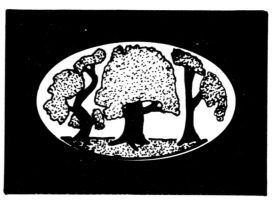

The emblem of the 12th Corps, worn as a sleeve badge, showed the oak, the ash and the thorn.

9 They also serve . . .

The next period for the coast gunners could rightly be termed 'They also serve who only stand and wait'. Admittedly life in the batteries had now changed. Whilst some effort was still directed towards training, a certain tenseness developed, as each man realised just how important his job had now become, in the matter of a few days. It was no longer a joke to see if one could head the layer's competition each week, or to see how many rounds one could get through the dummy loader, quite regardless of drill or reality. It was now a case of getting as much sleep as possible during the day, and remaining very much alert at night.

When the alarm bells rang, as they frequently did, everybody turned out, whether off duty or not. All spare men, not on duty, had posts assigned to them. The off duty watches went straight to the magazines, to expedite the flow of shells and cartridges to the guns, and all other men went to allocated positions round the battery perimeter. All guns, including the machine-guns were loaded and all searchlights exposed. These alarms were false, usually brought about by a nervous look-out or an over-zealous sentry. There was no direct attack on the port although the enemy on many occasions laid mines in the path of vessels approaching the entrances and on one occasion I saw two torpedoes, obviously fired at the entrance, miss their objective and hit the beach below Langdon Stairs, with a tremendous explosion. On that occasion, we were lucky not to lose our two fighting lights, which were sited close by. Every time these alarms sounded, we wondered whether this was it. There was no time to investigate, and if the enemy was here, the attack would open in a matter of seconds. The alarms were exhausting and frustrating, but it was better to be safe than sorry. Most of the men went to bed, semi-dressed, so that they could turn out quickly, whilst the officers, both of us, worked an irregular roster of about 24 hours on and 24 hours off, but we did not remove our uniforms at all, for at least six weeks. During the day, if it was clear weather, the off duty officer would organise training and do the general administrative duties of the battery. The other officer always remained inside the battery observation post, and close to the fire command telephone, having his meals sent up to him. We would, however, relieve one and another during the day, to break the monotony, and by mutual arrangement, and even during official night as it was then called. We only had one small camp-bed between us, so the arrangement seemed to work out all right. This was the position on the Eastern Arm, and the other batteries surrounding the harbour had similar arrangements. With more than two officers, however, it was possible to organise a better roster.

Each half hour during both the day and night, the tide was phoned down by the fire commander, who obtained his information from Pier Extension Battery. The tide had to be applied to the cam of the auto-sight, and this in itself helped to break the boredom during the night. The examination battery had a little more activity, in as much as it was engaged in reading signals, and firing its bring to round, if necessary. It is remarkable that about this time, the No. 2 gun at Langdon was adopted by a ginger cat. Nobody seemed to claim him and nobody knew where he came from. The troops decided to call him 'Whiskey' and each watch ensured that he was fed, and made a fuss of him. This peculiar cat was by no means gun shy, and even when the 6 inch gun went into action, he positioned himself to the rear of the gun, and not far away. I am sure he was an army cat with long artillery traditions, and he liked the smell of the cordite. He made his home actually on the gun floor of No. 2 gun, and certainly nobody disturbed him.

The battery strengths were now being increased considerably, to meet the revised establishments. Officers were being called up from Army Emergency Reserve and the Territorial Army Reserve of Officers. By August, Eastern Arm strength had been increased to three officers and 71 other ranks, Langdon to five officers and 126 other ranks, Pier Turret to three officers and 86 other ranks, Pier Extension to 3 officers and 57 other ranks, South Breakwater to three officers and 86 other ranks, whilst Citadel had five officers and 140 other ranks. The Fire Command Post had three officers and 18 telephonists and signallers. The

Corps Commander of Coastal Artillery, Brigadier C. W. Raw showing a dummy loader shell to America's roving ambassador, Wendell Willkie. The author is wearing a forage cap on the right.

regimental commander, when not engaged in administrative duties at the R.H.Q. in Cliff Block, would also help out in the F.C.'s duties. The administrative block consisted of a number of drivers, dispatch riders, clerks, the adjutant and the regimental sergeant major, but the R.Q.M.S. and ration stores remained housed in Langdon Barracks. There was a group of bungalows, known as Broadleas, at the foot of Langdon, and on the north-east side of the North Foreland meadow, which housed a number of women of the Auxiliary Territorial Service. These served as drivers, clerks and later, I believe, manned some of the anti-aircraft guns. Incidentally, a plan was drawn up that in the event of an enemy raid, or invasion, all the A.T.S. girls, together with the Langdon Barracks staff, were to retreat immediately to within the Langdon Battery perimeter.

With the expansion of the defences, and the siting of new batteries around the port and other major defended areas, it became obvious that the administration and control at present in the hands of the Commander, Royal Artillery, who in turn was directly responsible to the G.O.C., had become too heavy and cumbersome, and in urgent need of delegation. Until 1940, it was sufficient for a commander fixed defences to command major ports, but with the appointment of a corps commander, and a vital area of the coast now open to attack, it was preferable that a coast gunner, with specialised knowledge of coast defences, should be appointed. He would be directly responsible to the C.C.R.A., in just the same way as a C.R.A. was responsible to a divisional commander. As I have already stated, our own regimental commander, formerly battery commander of 168 Heavy Battery, Dover, was appointed C.C.C.A. Lt. Col. C. W. Raw was now promoted to Brigadier, and given a job which in itself was a compliment to the Territorial gunners. His area ran from Herne Bay in the East to Dungeness in the West. A staff was provided, and the headquarters were set up in the old casemates beneath Dover Castle. These casemates consisted of long winding tunnels, cut through the chalk, some 100 feet below the surface. They were air conditioned, and had many large spacious rooms, ideal for the purpose of an operations room and military headquarters. They were occupied not only by the army, but the navy had their headquarters there, under the command of the Vice Admiral Dover, Admiral Sir B. H. Ramsay, later by Vice Admiral Pridham Whippell. The anti-aircraft had their operation network set up in the casemates and R.A.F. representatives were also present. There was accordingly, a complete liaison between all the services, particularly the navy and coast artillery. The closest co-operation possible was essential between these two services as it was later to be proved, when the heavier artillery guns were used to support light naval forces in the channel.

The casemates could be reached either by a spiral staircase, near Cliff Block, or by a long sloping tunnel whose entrance came out near the old, long, disused Leg of Mutton Battery, by Canon's Gate. The rooms were safe from aerial attack, and planning could continue uninterrupted during the heaviest bombardment. They also had the advantage of having small balconies, so the occupants could, if they wished, have a

clear view of the harbour and channel. Later in the war, all radar information was collected in these operation rooms, and when the great batteries of Wanston and South Foreland were in action, they were able to provide cover for the M.T.B.'s engaged in attacking a target. Their exact position had to be known accurately by the batteries, so that they could lift their barrage just ahead of the naval forces.

The casemates were also later provided with a well equipped hospital, gas decontamination centre, a telephone exchange, Royal Engineer and Signal offices, and quarters for a host of clerks and telephonists. A.T.S. girls were used to man the operations table, showing the sea area of the channel and straits together with the position of all friendly and enemy craft. The table was of course marked out with the now familiar grid.

In fact it was not long before we had all the set up to defend the port and town, as far as communications and tactics were concerned, and we could contain a seige for as long a period as ammunition and food lasted. The Royal Engineer Tunnelling Companies, known as 'Moles' were for ever digging new tunnels at new depths, even up to the end of the war. The balconies and windows of the casemates can still be seen today, in the cliff below the fire command post, which still remains in Dover Castle.

An external portion of the headquarters beneath Dover Castle, giving a clear view of the harbour and channel. This photograph by The Dover Express was taken in 1980 and shows the Dover by-pass swinging round from the cliffs to the eastern docks where further extension work was under way.

If the enemy had laid seige to the town, and provided our batteries had not fallen into his hands, it was considered that the defence of the area was adequate and certainly the most efficient then available. The C.C.C.A. and the Admiral both had a clear picture of the straits with the arcs of fire of the batteries, with their extreme ranges, marked on the gridded table. It was possible therefore to put a battery in a state of instant readiness, as soon as a hostile plot approached its area, and the distribution of fire so set out, that it measured in some way to the old distribution of fire scheme we had earlier worked so hard to apply. Such a means of highly efficient and effective means of deployment of naval forces and guns was not available in early 1940, and was then dependent on information by telephone calls from the outer defences and the two rather vintage C.H.L. sets, M1 and M2, then considered the greatest break-through of detection and range finding of the century. Even these early radar sets were not operational until early 1941 and were then manned by coast artillery detachments. In 1940 when the invasion was imminent, the C.A. operations room combined with the navy was the most sophisticated means of defence then devised, and should Dover be beseiged or by-passed by invading forces, the control of the defences in the role of the now highly important C.A. supported by light naval forces, and some infantry battalions, was well co-ordinated.

However, after Dunkirk, there was one major issue which occupied the minds of the defence chiefs. First priority now had to be given to the build-up of the defences on the coast of south-east Kent, and just as important, the training of men to man the equipment. Guns would be of little use if they were not serviced by competent coast gunners. Another important issue was the siting of the new batteries. Unfortunately there was little reserve in the Coast Artillery store to equip the Emergency Batteries, as they were then called. Through the intervention of the Prime Minister, however, the navy once again came to the rescue. They released from their stores guns and mountings, as well as ammunition, held spare or removed from some of H.M. Ships. It was said that even the four six inch guns mounted on the Leas at Folkestone, at one time were mounted on *H.M.S. Hood.*

As far as the port of Dover was concerned, it was decided to supplement the six inch fire power by installing three six inch guns on the Western Heights, below and just east of the Citadel complex, and near what was formerly the old St. Martin's battery. The only rangefinder available was a Dumaresque, not nearly so accurate as the Barr & Stroud or our own position finders. Nevertheless this was all that could be spared, and in the event of a major attack by many vessels, it would certainly have served its purpose. The battery itself was designated Western Heights Battery and was ready for action in the latter part of 1940. Also it was decided to reinforce the defences guarding the eastern entrance, and two four inch guns were installed on the Knuckle. A battery was moved down from the Orkneys to man them. Lydden Spout was equipped with three six inch guns, followed by Capel Battery, with three eight inch guns, and Hougham Battery, between Lydden Spout and Citadel, with three eight inch guns. It was now decided to bring Capel, Hougham, Lydden Spout, and Citadel together under one regiment, having its own fire command post, and named 520 Coast Regiment, the Dover defences still being designated 519 Coast Regiment. The Prime Minister was anxious that even larger guns must be installed and so the birth of 540 Coast Regiment, embracing the two fifteen inch, four nine point two guns and three six inch guns at Fan Bay, close to Langdon. There was additional help from the Royal Marines, but more of these batteries in a later chapter.

Meanwhile, Brigadier Raw, together with Brigadier Burrowes, and their advisers were surveying the area of invasion for suitable sites, and as a result, emergency batteries of six inch were installed at Herne Bay, Margate, Kingsgate, Joss Bay, Sandwich Bay, Sandown Castle (Deal), Deal Castle, Kingsdown, St. Margarets Bay (four 5.5 inch), Folkestone, Mill Point (four 5.5 inch), Hythe, Dumpton Point, Dymchurch, Littlestone, Dungeness, Jury's Gut, and Greatstone. There were insufficient searchlights to service these batteries, and accordingly a variety of systems were used to make up for this deficiency. For instance, portable and highly polished reflectors were set up, and magnesium flares burnt in front giving off a bright light, which unfortunately lightened up all the surrounding area, making it vulnerable to air attack. They were not easy to traverse and were called Ryder's Flares. Another very similar system was known as Lion's Flares. When experimenting with such a light, at Mill Point, near Hythe, shortly after the bright illumination was made, the battery was attacked by aircraft. Although they did little damage, it was an indication of the weakness of such a system, and the vulnerability of the batteries. The Coast Training Regiments were also doing their best, and working at very high pressure to turn out coast gunners; even some of the infantry companies were converted in the desperate attempt to put up a shield against the enemy and to endeavour to stop a landing. Whilst these emergency batteries would, no doubt, have acquitted themselves well had the need arisen, they were too vulnerable both to attack by land and air, and it would not have been long before they would have been over-run. The amount of damage they could have inflicted upon the enemy would have been insignificant, especially in the flat Dungeness marshes, and a determined attempt to land in this area would very shortly have overcome any resistance the emergency batteries could have offered. On the other hand, with the enemy but 21 miles away and facing us on the Calais cliffs, it would have been extremely negligent not to have taken these measures, as there was little else to prevent a determined enemy reaching London. In July to September, 1940, once having breached the beach defences, the enemy would only have to contend with guerilla warfare, however formidable, on his road to London. Whether he would have been prepared to by-pass the fortress of Dover, which could seriously interrupt his lines of supply, remains an unanswered question.

In January, 1941, Mr. Churchill in a memo to General Ismay expressed considerable concern in the delay in installing the large batteries at Dover, and he then called for a weekly report on the progress of their installation. After visiting our own C.C.C.A. Brigadier Raw in February, 1941, the Prime Minister expressed even greater annoyance at the delay in a memo to no less a person than the Assistant Chief to the Imperial General Staff.

From our position at Langdon we watched the progress of the new battery at Fan Bay. The barbed wire surrounding Langdon was now about 30 feet thick, but by means of a staggered path through the wire,

just wide enough to take one person, we could pass with little difficulty into the gap, known as Langdon Hole, and watch the excavations and all the building work then in progress, something which we had never seen on such a large scale before. There were many speculative rumours amongst the troops, on the size and purpose of these new earthworks. The purpose of our path through the wire was to shorten the journey to the narrow zig-zag path, which went down the cliff to the fighting lights below. There was in fact a small beach, just below these lights, which could provide the landing place for a small body of the enemy, perhaps a commando raid, to destroy these installations or a raid on the battery, so the path was carefully protected by barrels, containing water and oil, which could be ignited by a rifle shot. This would certainly delay an enemy for a short time, but the weakness lay in the fact that he would

The Prime Minister, Winston Churchill, and the Corps Commander, General Bernard Montgomery, on a tour of inspection of Fan Bay Battery in 1941.

probably reach the top of the cliff before we even spotted him. As our early warning, we were relying on a telephone direct to the fighting lights, but in all probability the operators would have been quietly silenced before they could give any alarm.

Langdon Hole was used for another purpose also. A range was built for training with a spigot mortar. A wire was stretched across the upper end of the Hole, and an object, fixed to the wire, dragged across to represent an armoured vehicle. Our old mortar was sited near the edge of the cliff, and hurled its large and somewhat cumbersome projectile at the moving target. I never recorded a hit during the time I watched and fired this additional means of defence, but it provided amusement and a break from the usual training.

A Spigot Mortar had a maximum range of 822 metres with a bomb weighing 9·07kgs.

10 The opposition

Since the fall of France, and the occupation of the French coastal ports, it was obvious that the German's next move must be the preparation for the eventual invasion of Britain. Hitler, like Napoleon before him, would require command of the English Channel for a minimum period of 24 hours, although 48 hours was the time later demanded. Napoleon only required the removal of the English ships from the Strait for this period, but Hitler would also require the removal of the English planes from the sky, for the same period. The German staff demanded that, before they could commit their ships to any channel venture, and more especially if they were required to escort slow moving barges and tugs, an air umbrella, free from any serious diversion by a defeated Royal Air Force, would be essential. They had the assurance of Reichsmarschall Hermann Goering that the German air force would soon have mastery of the air, and the British airfields, on the southern coast at least, would be rendered useless by continuous bombing. And so plans were submitted by the German High Command on the requirements for the operation to be code-named 'Sea Lion'.*

Originally, the German plan was to invade with medium sized ships of 4000 to 5000 tons and numerous small craft. It was then the view of the British First Sea Lord, Admiral Pound, that a total of 100,000 men might well reach our shores without being seriously intercepted by our naval forces, but the maintenance and supply of these forces would be practically impossible, unless the R.A.F. and navy were completely overwhelmed and the coast batteries annihilated.

It was also observed that the Germans had commenced building sites for heavy batteries and a concentration of very large guns was seen along the cliffs between Blanc Nez and Griz Nez. These batteries, it was considered, would be added to and made capable of bombarding the channel ports, and also provide covering fire for an invading fleet. Mr. Churchill was soon concerned over this additional menace, which was rapidly taking shape during the months of August and September, and he felt that some effort should be made to counter this fire power, preferably with guns. He therefore gave orders to General Lord Ismay, head of the military wing of the cabinet, that two 14 inch guns should be mounted for counter battery work, against the German batteries. This battery came into being in late 1940. The guns were manned by the

*As part of Operation Sea Lion planned for 1940, the men of the No. 4 Company of the Brandenburg Regiment, all English speaking and familiar with British ways, were to be landed with the first assault wave. Upon beaching one group was to mount bicycles and to ride up to the gun positions. The artillery positions were to be captured. A second group would simultaneously attack Dover Harbour to prevent the sinking of a blockship which was stationed at the entrance.

Royal Marine Siege Regiment, and aptly named 'Winnie' and 'Pooh'. They were heavily camouflaged, and positioned at St. Margarets-at-Cliffe. The speed and efficiency by which these guns came into being certainly impressed the Prime Minister. They could, however, never be an effective reply to the opposition, their rate of fire being much slower than their German counterparts, as well as the system of firing. They fired their first round in combat on 22nd August, 1940, and indeed made history, for this was the first occasion that a shell from England had landed on the shores of France. The stories in the press at the time, recording 'huge gun duels across the channel', could only have been put out for propaganda purposes and to improve morale. A couple of rounds from 'Winnie and Pooh', could by no stretch of the imagination match the eight gun salvoes fired from the German long range guns.

The erection of the German gun emplacements could clearly be observed from the Dover cliffs, and they caused the Prime Minister much concern. He felt that positive action should be taken to eliminate them, before they were ready for use. With this end in view, he sent a memo to the First Sea Lord suggesting that the old monitor ship, *H.M.S. Erebus*, mounting two 15 inch guns, be used to bombard the batteries, preferably by night. He took the matter up very urgently with the Admiralty on a number of occasions, but the *Erebus* was never used for this bombardment. It is possible that the Admiralty felt that they had already suffered heavy losses during the Dunkirk evacuation, and should an invasion take place in the near future, they would require every

Royal Marines cleaning the barrel of 'Winnie' or 'Pooh' at St. Margarets-at-Cliffe.

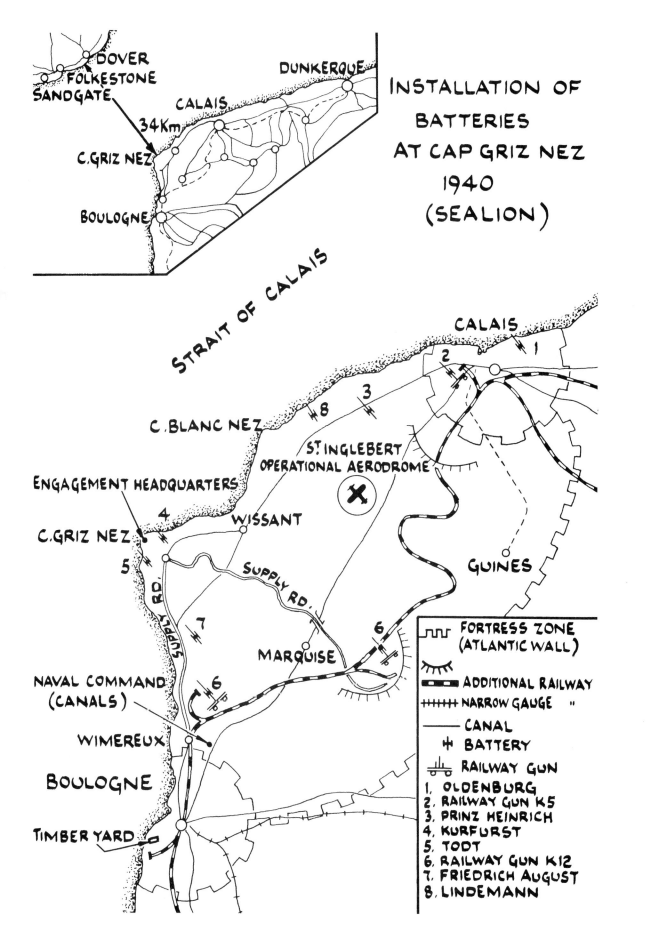

INSTALLATION OF
BATTERIES
AT CAP GRIZ NEZ
1940
(SEALION)

DOVER
FOLKESTONE
SANDGATE
34 Km
CALAIS
DUNKERQUE
C. GRIZ NEZ
BOULOGNE

STRAIT OF CALAIS

CALAIS

C. BLANC NEZ

 St. INGLEBERT
OPERATIONAL AERODROME

ENGAGEMENT HEADQUARTERS

C. GRIZ NEZ

WISSANT

GUINES

SUPPLY RD.

SUPPLY RD.

MARQUISE

NAVAL COMMAND
(CANALS)

WIMEREUX

BOULOGNE

TIMBER YARD

FORTRESS ZONE
(ATLANTIC WALL)

ADDITIONAL RAILWAY

NARROW GAUGE   "

CANAL

BATTERY

RAILWAY GUN

1. OLDENBURG
2. RAILWAY GUN K5
3. PRINZ HEINRICH
4. KURFURST
5. TODT
6. RAILWAY GUN K12
7. FRIEDRICH AUGUST
8. LINDEMANN

available ship; it was a far too hazardous undertaking to risk the *Erebus* in narrow waters for a purpose which could only be temporary.

By September, 1940, one of the largest German batteries was ready for action. This was the SIEGFRIED BATTERY, just south of Cap Gris Nez and mounting four 38 cm guns. This was quickly followed by: —

FRIEDRICH-AUGUST BATTERY, north of Boulogne mounting three 30.5 cm guns.

GROSSER KURFURST on Cap Gris Nez mounting four 28 cm guns.

PRINZ HEINRICH BATTERY west of Calais mounting two 21 cm guns.

OLDENBURG BATTERY in Calais area mounting two 21 cm guns.

LINDEMANN BATTERY between Cap Blanc Nez and Calais mounting three 40.6 cm guns.

TODT BATTERY near Cap Gris Nez mounting four 38 cm guns.

In addition, the Germans brought up a number of railway mounted guns, capable of firing across the Strait. The 40 cm guns were, in fact, equivalent to 16 inch guns, and the 28 cm approximately 11 inch. It was reported that the Germans, not unlike our own emergency measures, had taken some of the big coast artillery guns from the French naval warships in their hands, including the battleship *Jean Bart*.

This was, indeed, a very formidable array, and was in fact, the beginning of the great Atlantic Wall, built by the so-called Todt workers. The British had no answer to such a barrage, and our reply for the time being could only be token, through the good offices of the Royal Marines and Winnie and Pooh. However, the purpose uppermost in the minds of the defence chiefs was not counter battery work, but the defence of this particular sector against invasion. Mr. Churchill, on a number of occasions, reiterated that the channel must be closed to all German shipping, just as every attempt would be made by the Germans to close the straits to all British shipping, and, more important, we must have effective means of being able to do so.

Slowly the great formation of German guns took place. They were protected by a huge shield of concrete, some fifteen feet thick in places, which provided ample cover against air attack, but had the disadvantage of restricting their arc of fire. They had a limited traverse, only across the channel; but it seemed extremely unlikely that they would ever be required to fire in any other direction, and consequently the limited arc was not considered to be any great disadvantage.

Another feature of these huge gun protecting walls were the holes left in the rear of the blast wall. They were afraid that the back pressure from the muzzle might affect the gun detachments. They found, however, that this proved to be fallacious, so filled in the holes with brick, and not reinforced concrete, as the remaining part of the shield. The French Resistance Movement already had pictures of these holes, and when the Canadian tanks arrived and attacked the batteries, they simply had to fire anti-tank shells through the weakened bricked-up holes, knowing exactly were they were, and then put flame-throwers through the holes to the extreme discomfort of the gun detachments, who imagined themselves well protected by the thick concrete surround.

This diagram is copied from German plans and shows the Todt Battery.

TODT BATTERY (38 cm)

1 & 2 - AMMUNITION DUG-OUT.
3 & 4 - GUN CREWS DUG-OUT.
✚ FIRST AID DUG-OUT

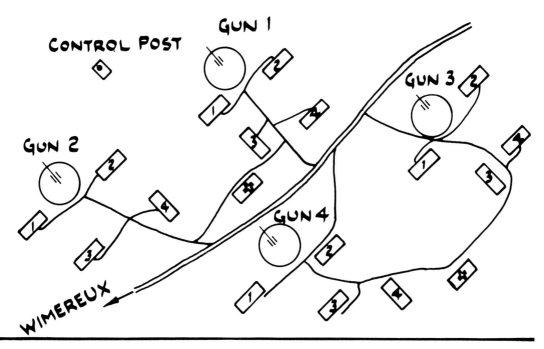

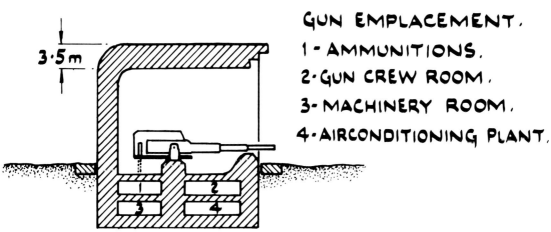

GUN EMPLACEMENT.
1 - AMMUNITIONS.
2 - GUN CREW ROOM.
3 - MACHINERY ROOM.
4 - AIRCONDITIONING PLANT.

CONTROL POST

DUG-OUTS

An interesting point however, was revealed after the war and is worth noting at this stage. Korvetten Kapitan Kurt Schilling, a rank equivalent to Captain (Navy) in the Reserve, commanded, administratively, all the marine group of guns, which included Battery Todt (38 cm), Grosser Kurfurst (28 cm) on Cap Gris Nez and other batteries between Boulogne and Calais. He also had operational control of fire of Lindemann Battery (40.6 cm) and some nearby railway guns. Some years after the war, when contact had been made with him, by an artillery officer from the British 540 Coast Regiment, he stated that in the days before the batteries were captured by the Canadians, he received orders not to spike the guns. It would appear that the German High Command, anticipating a complete breakthrough in the Ardennes by Field Marshal von Runstedt in December, 1944, would fight back to the channel ports and recapture the guns.

By 5th June, the evacuation of the troops from Dunkirk had been completed, and by 22nd June, France had surrendered, so now we were completely alone in facing the continent, and were only heartened and inspired by the fine speeches of defiance by the Prime Minister. I repeat that we were absolutely confident that we could resist any invasion fleet that Hitler was likely to launch against us, but history has since revealed that our task might not have been so easy as we supposed.

Field Marshal Rommel visiting the defences with Captain Kurt Schilling who was in charge of the Calais batteries in 1944.

The plan to attack England, Operation Sea Lion, was changed many times, mainly due to the differences of opinion by the German chiefs of staff. The original plan was perfectly straightforward. Under cover of continuous bombardment of our coast defences by their long range guns, and after the now familiar process of softening up by the Luftwaffe, it was proposed to launch a concentrated invasion fleet through a narrow corridor, and by the shortest sea route. The corridor would be protected by small units of the German navy and by submarines. The German navy felt, however, that they could not be responsible for the sole protection of the corridor, especially after their loss of ships, and their experience in the Norway invasion. The army was reluctant to trust itself without firm guarantees from both the navy and the Luftwaffe, and so it seemed that only after achieving complete mastery of the air could any guarantees be acceptable. Without air supremacy, sea supremacy could not be assured, and it was possible that the whole army would be destroyed. Certainly its lines of communication would be precarious, even if they managed to make a beach head. Admiral Raeder was not prepared to accept these conditions, and so the preliminary plan was abandoned. Hitler, however, was insistent that the most effective way of bringing the war to a speedy conclusion was Sea Lion, and especially before the United States of America could be persuaded by Mr. Churchill, either to replace all the British lost arms after Dunkirk, or even enter the war herself.

Other plans were therefore drawn up by the high command, and submitted to Hitler. Various points of view were put forward, from landing troops between Ramsgate and Dover, or on a broader front such as North Foreland to the Isle of Wight. The shipping available to the Germans had to be considered as a major controlling influence, and it was felt possible that sufficient ships, made up of small landing craft, barges, and all commandeered vessels in all the now occupied countries, could carry about 100,000 men in the first wave. This would have to be followed up by a further 150,000 men in support, bringing the total to $\frac{1}{4}$ million fully armed men and equipment, to be landed within a space of two or three days. The sea and air corridor would have to be kept open for at least this period of time. It was calculated that 170 transports, 1900 barges, 400 tugs, and 1600 motor boats of various sizes and description would be available to act as the ferries.

The German army staff was bitterly opposed to such an attack on such a broad front and felt that the risk involved was too great. They felt that the losses in such a venture would be colossal, as the British would throw in everything they had left, regardless of the cost. Should the attack fail or be only partially successful, the loss of face to the Germans in the eyes of the remaining and uncommitted world would be immeasurable. It would appear that the so far invincible German army could be beaten, and it would lend heart to every country still opposed to them, or half heartedly neutral. Any plan therefore, must be cast iron and guaranteed to ensure sufficient numbers of troops could be landed, supported by reserves to consolidate a firm beach head and capture a port within the shortest space of time. The problems differed very little from those facing the allies in 1944, except that complete domination of the air and

sea was then assured, whereas the Germans could reckon on no such guarantee. The objective must be a suitable landing ground, which could be reasonably defended against a spirited counter attack, a harbour or small port, to facilitate the landing of the heavier equipment and tanks, as well as provide suitable piers or moles for the deeper draft ships. Finally the landed troops should have a reasonable chance of advancing to or encircling the capital.

Finally a compromise plan was drawn up reluctantly by the chiefs of staff of both army and navy and on the insistence of Hitler. Time was fast running out, and the invasion should be under way by the end of August. Any attack on Dover by seaborne forces was abandoned. It was considered that our firepower was too great, and a heavy loss of men, ships, and materials would result from any attempt to capture the harbour in a frontal assault. (It is a pity we did not know this at the time.) In the harbour batteries, we did receive intelligence reports, two or three times a week. These were compiled by the R.A.F. under the title of Jim Crow and P.R.U. (Patrol Reconnaissance Unit), whose task it was to photograph the French and Belgium ports. These reports were alarming in themselves, and on the Eastern Arm I saw no reason to convey the contents to all ranks. The reports contained information on the number and concentration of barges and landing craft, transports, tugs and converted types of vessels, in the ports of Calais, Boulogne, Gravelines, Dunkirk and numerous other small French and Belgium ports. Photographs also showed larger barges coming down from Cuxhaven, Bremen, Kiel, Hamburg, Amsterdam, and even as far away

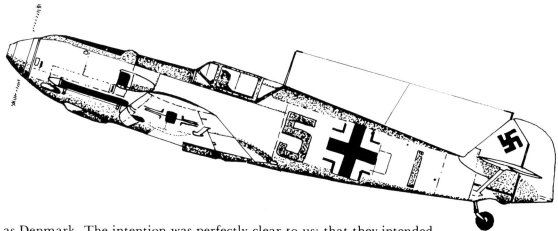

as Denmark. The intention was perfectly clear to us: that they intended to attack by the shortest possible sea route, with the maximum ships available, and that we would be the first objective. The R.A.F. concentrated their bombing raids on these ports, and at night we could clearly see the bomb flashes and tracer bullets in the sky along the French coast. There is no doubt that many vessels were destroyed by the R.A.F., and it made a severe hindrance to the troops engaged in boarding practice. The build up became quite intensive, and it could have done little to boost the morale of the German troops quartered in the vicinity of the ports, to see each morning yet another trail of destruction of their transports, by an air force which was supposed to be annihilated.

The German command considered that they had provided for such losses and as far as they were concerned, it now rested on the Luftwaffe and its ability to protect the troops in transit. It was quite obvious from the attacks on the French ports that the striking power of the R.A.F. had not been seriously impaired and it was essential that it be deflated and demoralised, before the invasion could commence. Complete mastery of the air was essential and this was realised by both attacker and defender alike. Goering knew he must have the whip hand, at least over South-East England, for a few days, and this could only be brought about by the destruction of the airfields and landing strips, where these coastal defenders were based. The Luftwaffe units, based in Northern France and in the Pas de Calais area, consisted mainly of Junkers 87 dive bombers, Junkers 88, Dornier D.O. 17, and Messerschmitts 109, with a few Heinkels. The pattern was clear and in the months of July and August, and mid September, the raids all along the south-east and southern England were prolonged and vicious. All sea traffic, whether it be naval or merchantman, was attacked, airfields were bombarded almost out of recognition, and the R.A.F. were engaged constantly and without respite. Whilst the R.A.F. suffered severe losses, both on the ground and in the air, and their Spitfires and Hurricanes were outnumbered in nearly all the aerial combats. German losses were even greater, and whereas many British airmen were able to land safely on their own soil, the enemy loss in pilots continued to be a heavy drain on the German resources.

The Messerschmitt 109E was a single-seater fighter with a maximum speed of 348 m.p.h., and a range of 400 miles.

By August, 1940, Colonel-General Halder and the chief of the German naval staff, together with Hitler, agreed that to attack on a broad front along the whole of the south coast would be suicidal. Landings between Deal and Ramsgate were abandoned, and likewise no attempt would be made to land troops in the Dover area. It was finally decided, not without considerable misgivings, that the German 16th Army would land in the area of Folkestone, Hythe, Rye, Hastings, and Eastbourne, and the German 9th Army, sailing from Boulogne and Le Harve, would land in Brighton and Bognor areas. The 16th Army would turn east on landing and capture Dover on the landwards side, then having linked up with the 9th Army, establish a line between Canterbury and Arundel. In all, some eleven divisions would be landed in the initial attack, and in the next few days they would be supported by further divisions from the 6th Army, being held in reserve. Portsmouth was to be taken, and then the line advanced towards London in an encircling movement from Gravesend, through Redhill, Reigate and Guildford. The date fixed for the landings was 15th September, but was later advanced to 21st September.

Now the plan was ready, the German chiefs of staff turned their eyes to the Reichsmarschall Goering. It was vital that the R.A.F. be subdued, at least in this corner of the world, to enable this vast armada to sail. It had already suffered some losses at the embarkation points, from the hands of the British airforce, but as these losses had already been allowed for in the original estimates, a fighting force of men and machines, considered sufficient enough to overwhelm all British resistance on the foreshore and later in the countryside, had been assembled. As Hitler had remarked, it would not just be a country drive through the pretty English lanes and byways. Once a man is fighting on his own soil for his own homestead, the fiercer he will resist. It was estimated that every crossroad, defile and village, would be defended, and it was expected that losses on both sides would be very heavy indeed. The German high command felt, however, that superior numbers of well trained troops and superior arms must in time prevail. Once London was occupied, all British resistance would cease. They did not reckon on a Churchill surrender, but simply a change of government, willing to come to terms, possibly, but not necessarily led by a quisling. Although it was thought that every endeavour would be made to obtain favourable conditions, before complete surrender, the British could not expect much mercy from the hands of the invaders, in view of the trouble they had caused, and they would have little sympathy for the Jewish community, many of whom in the late 1930's had fled from Germany. If they could catch Churchill, so much the better, but they realised he was quite capable of organising a guerilla type warfare, the seat of government, together with the remains of the fleet, being transferred to Canada.

So the battle for Britain commenced from the end of June, and was to rage until nearly the end of September. After then the tides and weather conditions would be unfavourable, and it would be inadvisable to keep the vast armada in concentrated form during the winter months, exposed to air attack. If air supremacy was not established, all ideas of

A cartoon by C. King in 1944 depicting the part played by Air Sea Rescue boats in saving the lives of pilots and sailors in the Strait of Dover.

invasion would have to be postponed until 1941, and the end of the war put back until then.

Command of the air above the Channel was the vital link, and Reichsmarschall Goering had promised it. The full story of the Battle of Britain has been written elsewhere, but it is sufficient to relate how it was fought over Dover.

Increased aerial activity over the Channel was now observed and on 1st July, the local anti-aircraft shot down its first Dornier. Attacks on the port and channel shipping were to intensify, as well as attacks on the harbour defences and batteries. Long ranged guns, soon to be about 40 in number, E-boats, R-boats, and similar fast moving craft, were now patrolling the Channel, ready to torpedo any target which might present itself. An air force, superior in numbers, was determined to gain dominance in the skies, across this narrow strip of water, long enough to ensure the safe passage of the vast mass of ships, laden with troops, tanks and guns. The victorious Wehrmacht were waiting to follow in the paths of Julius Caesar, William of Normandy and Eustace the Monk. Hitler saw the problem through the same eyes as Napoleon. Both had stood on the cliffs near Boulogne and viewed the white cliffs of Dover, so tantalisingly near and yet so far. This same strip of water must be controlled by the invaders, before it was safe to attempt a crossing, but always the same question was uppermost in the minds of the leaders of France and Germany . . . how?

11 More waiting

Meanwhile and immediately after the Dunkirk evacuation, everybody realised that preparations were going ahead for an invasion but nobody knew what the plan would be, and in spite of many speculations, nobody could forecast with any degree of accuracy where the landings would be attempted.

Feverish activity was raging, not only in the town itself, but also in the batteries and the environment. Certain preparations we had made have already been described in an earlier chapter, but I would again emphasise that an extraordinary feeling of confidence was felt everywhere and nowhere was any feeling of despondency expressed. We were almost eager to put our little schemes to the test, and everyone was sure that the town of Dover and its port would not be occupied by a foreign foe, and certainly not the Eastern Arm.

However one disconcerting element was conveyed to me by a friend who had been transferred to the 5th Super Heavy Regiment, a battery of two 12 inch guns stationed near Shepherdswell tunnel. In the event of a landing by enemy troops on the piers or moles, the duty of his battery was to engage them and neutralise the harbour installations, including me!

On 5th July, 1940, a directive from Mr. Churchill to General Ismay stated that clear instructions should now be issued to the people of Dover to the effect that all non-essential townsfolk should evacuate the town. They should be encouraged to leave voluntarily, and although no compulsory order had been issued, it could be imposed if it was later considered necessary. Propaganda to be circulated by the regional commissioner would be directed to this end. All doubtful elements, and by this it was meant all persons who might have the slightest sympathy with the Nazi cause, or feel that a useful purpose would be served by making peace and coming to terms with Hitler, were to be removed immediately. The police had a list of such sympathisers, and they would be arrested as soon as it was felt that they might give assistance to the enemy. Those people who decided to remain in Dover because of business or family ties and those still carrying out essential services, were instructed to go to air raid shelters and caves, and remain there until the battle was over. There would be no question of refugees cluttering up the roads, as had happened in France and Belgium and the defenders must not be impeded in any way. In point of fact, the pre-war population of

Typical of the many shows put on at the Hippodrome, the nearest theatre to occupied Europe. This show on 19th December, 1943 was sponsored by the 520 Coast Regiment R.A.

Dover was about 38,000 and during the invasion period it fell to under 16,000. Many of the persons remaining were shopkeepers and publicans and their families, and other persons necessary to maintain the minimum life standards of the port. Rows of houses now stood empty and likewise the streets. The bustle of a busy port, town and garrison had gone, and khaki and navy blue were very much the order of the day. There were no serious cases of looting reported on the empty houses, and every endeavour was made by the police, the mayor and his aldermen and councillors, to uphold morale and to keep the town alive, and to render every assistance by way of welfare and benefit to those who were now committed to defending it. Welfare centres were set up, and local solicitors attended by rota, giving their services free to those in need of help. The local Hippodrome in Snargate Street provided a variety of

ROYAL HIPPODROME DOVER .

SOUVENIR PROGRAMME .

— you lucky people

— an all star variety concert, presented by TOMMY TRINDER and a distinguished company,

— in aid of the ROYAL ARTILLERY PRISONERS OF WAR FUND .

entertainment, as did the cinemas which all remained open. The Dover Club which temporarily amalgamated with the Royal Cinque Ports Yacht Club, and situated in the centre of the seafront, remained open throughout the war, although the building was somewhat battle-scarred by 1945. Also remaining open was a small guest house, the Shalimar, whose proprietresses were two elderly ladies. Their house was also situated in the centre of the seafront, close to the Dover Club. These ladies carried on as if the war was on the other side of the world. They remained completely unperturbed when 16 inch shells were falling in the harbour, only a few hundred yards from their front dining room, although all their windows had long since been blown in. Their courage and so called 'stiff upper lip' was an example to us all. I am sure they would have still have been there, prepared to serve morning coffee to any guest, if the Germans had come marching down the seafront or pouring ashore on the beach opposite their house. They remained completely oblivious to their own personal safety and unperturbed by shattered windows and falling walls in the holocaust about them.

Later on an Officers' Club was established in the former Conservative Club at the foot of Castle Hill and by 1943 a concert party, mainly gunners from 520 Regiment and calling themselves the White Cliff Revels, performed in the Hippodrome. A number of professional artists would give their services to entertain the troops, both in the batteries and in the Hippodrome. On one occasion, the White Cliff Revels were successful in obtaining the services of Sonny Hale, Tommy Trinder, Tessie O'Shea and other well known performers. Even the great strip artiste, Phyllis Dixie, who later performed at the Whitehall Theatre, London, gave the troops a very popular show. We also had a visit from Evelyn Laye, whose husband Frank Lawton was then serving in the forces, and she visited the Castle and attended a dance in the grounds of Dover College, where the navy had its headquarters.

The men in the batteries had little time to get bored, and the entertainment described above only became available when the threat of invasion had receded during the winter months. The increase in

'Front Line Knotting Class'. The author organised a knot instruction class for Fire Command Personnel and Telephonists in Dover Castle in 1941. Sailors in the Port War Signal Station, which was above the Fire Command Post, produced this cartoon.

personnel from the reserves and called-up men, now meant an intensification of training. The watches could now be divided into three, allowing men eight hours on duty, eight in reserve and eight hours off. During the reserve period, training was carried out. Layers competitions were held to stimulate interest. This merely consisted of the placing of a clinometer, an instrument for measuring angles, on the breech of a gun with a set quadrant elevation or angle. The layer was required to elevate the gun and then re-lay on a datum point as near as he could to the pre-set angle. There were dummy loader competitions, to see how many rounds could be loaded through a wooden loader. Gun detachments tried to get as many rounds as possible through in the space of a minute, often to the neglect of gun drill. On the 6 inch, the standard rate of fire for a good detachment was eight rounds per minute, but on the dummy loader a figure of sixteen rounds was not unusual. On the twin six a similar dummy loader was used and again, far many more rounds were claimed than could ever have been fired on the equipment itself. The breeches were constantly breaking, but owing to the good offices of the blacksmith aboard the naval supply vessel the *Sandhurst* alongside the Eastern Arm, repairs were soon effected.

During the winter months, the victualling of the Southern Breakwater was particularly difficult, as all supplies had to be transferred by boat, usually the old *Seymour Castle*, and the landing of bulky food and awkward supplies on slippery stone steps, with a sea running, sometimes ended in disaster and loss. The orderly officer on the Southern Breakwater was also required each day to visit the eastern end of the mole to the emplacements known as the Knuckle. Later these emplacements were to have four inch guns installed, but in the early days they only contained three searchlights and an engine room with three Lister engines to provide the power. The journey along the breakwater could be particularly hazardous on occasions, and a bicycle was provided for whoever made the journey. Apart from a number of bollards, there was no protecting rail, and it was a case of choosing a gap between the high waves, which swept right over the breakwater in wintertime, and then making a dash for it. Later it became even more dangerous, as by early 1941 German planes were constantly machine-gunning, during a sweep along the mole. It was not unknown for the high seas to sweep the 100 lb shells from the gun platforms and personnel with them. On very cold days a brick was placed in the breech of the 6 inch to prevent the obturation pads from freezing. The look-outs on each gun, during this weather, were permitted to stand within the gun shields for protection, provided they maintained a look-out through the gun ports, but any attack in such conditions was so improbable that it was really a waste of time. However, a vigil had to be maintained as it was just possible that aircraft would be spotted laying mines in the channel.

We were feeling very much in the front line, and it was not long before events were to prove it. We had already suffered one fatal casualty in early November, 1939, when a member from the Pier Turret Battery had been swept over the Admiralty Pier and drowned. On 5th July, 1940, the enemy took more precise action against a coast defence battery.

A number of bombs were aimed and dropped at the Knuckle end of the Breakwater (although at this time no guns had yet been installed). A man was badly wounded, but no damage was done to the searchlights or engine room. A copy of the War Diary of the Regiment for the ensuing few months gives some idea of the military action taken against the defences.

15th July, 1940
> *Langdon Battery.* Four bombs on huts at rear of guns. One hut destroyed. 1 killed, 4 wounded.

29th July
> All harbour batteries heavily dive-bombed by large force of enemy planes. (Over 120 planes) consisting of JU 87 dive-bombers, escorted by ME 109's. Harbour installations set on fire. Four enemy planes destroyed by Spitfires. 3 wounded.

30th July
> Balloon barrage put up over Dover. *Citadel Battery* engaged E-boats.

12th August
> Hostile shelling for first time.(This refers to the shelling of an east bound convoy, and although the target was bracketed, and later rounds fell inside the harbour, no damage was suffered by the ships or installations.) It is believed that an earlier proofing round fell into the town at the top of the Tower Hamlets district and a house was demolished. There was no report of any planes in the area at the time.

Langdon Battery. Machine-gunned by hostile planes. 1 wounded.

The balloon barrage was repeatedly attacked during this period. Also the harbour batteries were subjected to continuous machine-gunning. On the Eastern Arm, two planes regularly machine-gunned the battery between 8 a.m. and 9 a.m. each morning.

31st August
> All balloons over the town shot down.
> *Citadel Battery.* Engaged enemy E-boats.

4th September
> *Langdon Battery.* Engaged enemy seaplane, believed photographing the defences. Plane had landed on water for a few minutes.

8th September
> *Citadel Battery.* One bomb on No. 2 emplacement. No damage to gun.

9th September
> About 150 shells at westbound convoy. No apparent serious damage to ships.

15th September
> *Langdon Battery.* Three bombs hit battery. One ten yards in front of No. 1 gun, one behind No. 1 gun, one on huts. Two bombs on Langdon Barracks. 11 wounded.

24th September
> *Citadel Battery.* Twice engaged enemy E-boats.

15th October
> *Citadel and Langdon Batteries.* Twice engaged enemy E-boats.

18th October
> *Pier Turret Battery.* Shell fell on Sergeants' Mess. 2 killed, 3 wounded.
> *Citadel Battery.* Engaged E-boats.

29th October
> *Citadel Battery.* Twice engaged E-boats.

30th October
> *Langdon Battery.* No. 1 gun straddled by two gun salvo. 2 wounded.

30th October
> *Langdon Battery.* Three shells in front of B.O.P. 6 wounded.
> *Citadel Battery.* Engaged E-boats.
> 12 bombs on battery. Bridge leading across moat into battery was destroyed. Officers Mess badly damaged.

14th November
> *Pier Turret Battery, Pier Extension and South Breakwater Batteries.* Suffered damage from severe storm. (It was necessary to rig life-lines along battery to enable watches to change over with some degree of safety, A number of six inch shells were washed overboard, and waves breaking over the Pier Turret washed railway coach into sea.)

Shelling of Dover Harbour photographed from the Southern Breakwater. Note the wreck of H.M.S. War Sepoy, on left.

20th November
Southern Breakwater Battery. Heavy waves breaking over breakwater. Two men caught by Knuckle lighthouse. 1 drowned.

27th November
Eastern Arm Battery. Heavily shelled. One operator in No. 2 searchlight emplacement killed. (This was also a T.A. soldier whose relatives were still living locally. They were invited to visit the battery and whilst present, further shelling broke out compelling them to remain in the battery for some hours.) 1 killed.

30th November
Citadel Battery. Engaged E-boats.

21st December
South Breakwater Battery. Heavy shelling and battery frequently straddled. One shell hit cookhouse. Three C.A.S.L. emplacements hit and B.O.P. damaged. 6 wounded.

24th December
Langdon and Citadel Batteries. Engaged E-boats.

16th January, 1941
Breakwater Battery. M.V. Silver Wings swept on to sunken blockship in western entrance during bad weather and 29 personnel on board rescued without loss of life, due to courage of L/Bdr. G. A. Freeman, who managed to convey a life-line from the battery to the stricken boat. L/Bdr. Freeman commended in 12th Corps Orders.
(Three ships had been sunk in the western entrance to seal it from entry by any vessel larger than a small motor boat. In addition a spiked boom was placed across the entrance. One vessel, *H.M.S. War Sepoy*, a fleet auxiliary, was badly damaged during a bombing attack on the harbour. She was towed to the western entrance and sunk. Being empty and damaged, the tide soon washed her to a position at right angles to the mole, so it was necessary to mark her with a 'Wreck' buoy, as she had now become a danger to our own shipping.)

During the next six months, there was intermittent bombing and shelling all round the defences and on the town, which was now showing considerable signs of damage. The batteries were frequently bombed but little damage was done and no gun put out of action as a result of enemy action. All batteries engaged hostile aircraft with Lewis machine-guns, without visible effect and floating mines were exploded either by L.M.G. or primary armament.

It became necessary for the town to warn its citizens by differentiating between a bomb and shell attack on the town. This was done by using the normal siren for air warning and sounding it twice after a brief interval. So two air raid warnings together indicated a shell attack. Unfortunately it usually meant that the shell warning could not be sounded until after the first round had fallen.

1879 rounds were fired before the end of 1941 of which 501 rounds were fired at the harbour and batteries on the moles, 189 at coast batteries on the cliffs, and 1189 into the town.

5th July, 1941

Breakwater Battery. Shell fell 14 yards west of No. 1 gun. 1 wounded.

2nd October

Archcliffe Fort. Two bombs on engine room. 1 wounded.

16th November

Eastern Arm Battery. Heavy gale and high seas swept over battery. 1 drowned.

16th December

Pier Extension Battery. Bombing attack. 1 wounded.

Western Heights Battery. Nissen hut destroyed by bombs. 1 wounded.

The diary goes on, but now somewhat sketchy, as what earlier had been an event now became commonplace, and a number of both offensive and defensive actions are not recorded. There is an indication that there were frequent alarms, caused by the presence of E-boats and R-boats, a type of German motor torpedo boat. They would leave their Channel bases in quite considerable numbers to sweep the Channel and attack allied shipping. The results of the engagements with these vessels by the defences is not known, and no claims at this stage could be made for a 'sinking'. The radar equipment was not sufficiently advanced to record fall of shot. The Royal Navy, with its own striking force of motor torpedo boats and motor gun-boats, played an extremely important role in not only providing escort duties, but also engaging the hostile boats, which were only too often superior in number. From the batteries we could see the tracer bullets flashing between two vessels as they engaged one another, and stories sometimes came ashore describing hand-to-hand fighting as vessels actually drew alongside one another.

The defences always had a good warning of the approach of an eastbound or westbound allied convoy, and the number of ships, by a code known as 'Kipis'. This would indicate that a shell attack on the convoy could be expected and would continue until the convoy was out of range. The firing of the German guns gave the flash spotters and sound rangers, forerunners of the modern locating regiments, an opportunity of obtaining a pinpoint on the gun flashes, and so calculate an accurate position, range and bearing of the enemy guns. The time of flight was about 58 seconds and the angle of descent of the shell, a steep one. The look-outs, when they observed the flashes, would start a stop watch, and after about 54 seconds, call out for all to duck, a moment or so before the salvoes landed. The shells would splinter, and it was these splinters which caused the the major amount of casualties. On occasions, the Germans tried air bursts over the town and defences, and although somewhat frightening, were no more effective.

On 27th July, 1940, we witnessed, to our sorrow, the loss of the now familiar destroyer, *H.M.S. Codrington.* She had been lying alongside *H.M.S. Sandhurst,* the R.N. supply ship, moored alongside the Eastern Arm, when the harbour was attacked by a number of Heinkels. A salvo

The destroyer 'Codrington' was sunk by Heinkel bombers. The supply ship 'Sandhurst' moored beside the Eastern Arm was also damaged. Note the pylons which used to carry buckets of coal on wires from Tilmanstone colliery to the loading points on the Eastern Arm. The carrying wires seem to have suffered in the raid.

of bombs fell in the sea close by the *Codrington* and the resultant explosion appeared to break her back. She settled down in the sea, near the Camber, obviously beyond all repair. The *Sandhurst* also was badly damaged, but managed to survive. Both vessels suffered a number of casualties.

Soon after, the navy decided that in view of the vulnerability of the destroyers based on Dover, and now being subjected, not only to air attack, but also shellfire, they would be withdrawn to a safer area, in Harwich and Sheerness, which also had the advantage of better air cover. *H.M.S. Boreas* and *H.M.S. Brilliant* had also been sunk in the Channel a few days earlier, just west of the port, whilst endeavouring to protect a convoy from air attack. It was a magnificent sight to see these fine ships, with all their guns firing, and tearing up and down the line of ships, like sheep dogs, protecting a flock from attackers. About 60 dive bombers had attacked the convoy, and were successful in sinking 5 ships and damaging about 4 or 5 more. Having been hit a number of times, it was a very sad sight to see these great ships, burning and settling down in the water, still firing with their few remaining guns, until they disappeared beneath the waves. We could do nothing to help them, but had to stand by helplessly. The price for keeping these valuable ships in Dover was too high, and so they had to go. The minesweepers sought some form of protection during a shell attack, by mooring alongside the breakwater, and at least they were fairly safe from splinters.

August 14th, 1940 saw another heavy attack on the harbour by over 100 Messerschmitts escorting nearly as many Junkers 87. This time they were engaged by about 50 Spitfires and Hurricanes. All the balloons of the barrage were shot down, but by a miracle little damage was done to the ships in the harbour or the installations or defences. A series of dog fights followed over the town and channel and at least 4 Junkers 87's were brought down within sight of us. Later two of these aircraft returned and sank a defenceless lightship.

On 7th September, 1940 the code word Cromwell was received and transmitted to all batteries. This was the warning that invasion was imminent. All batteries were required to 'Stand To'. On the Eastern Arm there seemed little point in disturbing the watch off duty and sleeping in the newly constructed wooden huts. All the guns of the defences were loaded. Additional trays of ammunition were brought up on the electric hoist on the Arm, and were stacked at the rear of the guns. We also primed all the hand grenades. These were issued to all ranks down to bombadier, but I retained half a dozen for myself, keeping two in my battledress pockets. Nothing happened during the night, and the look-outs were doubled. Next morning was a clear bright day and, in fact, we could see right across the channel to the French cliffs. Instead of a vast armada of ships approaching our shore, there was not a vessel in sight and certainly no invasion fleet coming to surprise us. It was not long afterwards that we received the signal to 'Stand Down' but remain alert, at least until mid October, when the chances of a successful invasion would become more remote. It was all rather an anti-climax.

Construction of the protecting concrete walls at the side of each equipment and the brick walls at the rear was now almost completed and this afforded the detachments protection against shell splinters and machine-gunning, and added much to their confidence.

By continuous shelling and bombing, the old port and town of Dover and many of its ancient landmarks were fast disappearing. The sea front houses, now deserted, were slowly being damaged beyond repair. Townwall Street and old St. James' Street and its near environment had been reduced to rubble. The Burlington Hotel had been badly damaged by shell-fire soon after the shelling commenced, and likewise the old church of St. James' received a direct hit. Many properties in Woolcomber Street suffered in the early part of the war.

The shell line, however, appeared to be through the centre of the town, through the market square, and the line direction seemed to be remarkably good and accurate. The bombing was less so, being more in the nature of quick raids as opposed to a concentrated bombing raids and whilst some casualties were suffered and some damage done, they were more of a nuisance value and not nearly so frightening as shelling. It was not long before Camden Crescent, the National Sailors' Home, (the anchor of the old *H.M.S. Vindictive* of Zeebrugge fame used to stand outside and was also destroyed), the Grand Hotel, by Granville Gardens and the bandstand, the Gordon Boys' Home, the Robin Hood Pub, and a number of other places familiar to Dovorians, including the well known Round House Club, were rendered uninhabitable, if not totally destroyed. Dover now became known in the world press as 'Shellfire Corner' and it certainly earned its name. Some protection from bombing was afforded by the balloon barrage, consisting of 18/20 balloons, although they seemed to provide target practice for Messerschmitt air gunners, and it was quite a common sight to see a burning balloon slowly sinking to the ground. One such balloon did not catch fire, but its fabric had been punctured, probably by shrapnel, and it sank down on the seawards side of the Eastern Arm Battery, together with all its equipage and tangled wire, etc. Every man who could be spared from the battery turned out to save it. We struggled and sweated all one afternoon to try and save it from sinking into the sea and so save the government a little money. Finally our efforts were rewarded, and we made it fast alongside and reasonably secure. We untangled all the wire and then sat back, well satisfied with our efforts. I rang up the balloon barrage people, who were a branch of the R.A.F. and triumphantly informed them that one of their balloons which they thought to be missing, had been saved, and would they come along and collect it. They merely replied 'Thanks very much, give it a cup of tea and turn it loose.' We were furious after all our efforts, and after two or three more phone calls, they eventually turned up. The balloon was apparently useless to them but they collected up all the ropes, etc. And so it was destroyed and cut up, the fabric being used for any purpose the possessor thought fit. I think we now had a tablecloth of silver in our mess for the first time. It made a change from the bare barrack table.

There was, however, a competition run amongst the local R.A.F. balloon barrage boys on the time it took to send up a replacement

The Market Square seconds after a shell landed in Market Street.
The town's damaged Fire Station. Note that 'Dover' has been blanked out for security reasons.
Old St. James' Church photographed by the 'Kent Messenger' in February 1945.

balloon, after one had been shot down. Whilst I have no note of the record time achieved, it was quite remarkable how soon a balloon sailed up into the sky, when shortly before it had come down blazing.

The local Territorials by now had made arrangements for sending away their families, as local wives were strongly discouraged by the corps commander. In the event of an attack, a man would always be looking over his shoulder to see which part of the town was suffering, but if he had no local connections, it would obviously not concern him quite so much.

We all realised that the Dover we knew pre-war, whatever happened, would never be the same again. One local hostelry which was popular with all ranks and remained open and unscathed throughout the war, was the Crypt or Shakespeare Bars. One could obtain a meal below ground level, in some degree of safety, whilst upstairs in the bars, all members of the forces, the R.N., minesweepers, R.A.F., fire spotters, and of course all the reporters from the national newspapers, foregathered for refreshment and a lot of shop was talked, notwithstanding the warning notices all round the walls. The Crypt was situated near the sea front and in the main street, and one could return to one's unit without much difficulty. It was said that at one time, if anybody forgot the password to re-enter Dover Castle, it could always be obtained from the barmaid at the Crypt. All entrances to the Castle were sealed off, except the entry by Canon's Gate, over which was mounted an infantry guard. The guardhouse was within the gate itself, and no doubt had been used by soldiers of Hubert de Burgh, many years ago. The sentry patrolled the drawbridge over the moat and was covered by another sentry by the gate itself. They were in fact armed with live ammunition, and there was no question of ceremony. An agent trying to enter could do a lot of damage, if he succeeded. If one visited the town at night, it was first necessary to obtain the password in order to get back, otherwise one would be landed in the guardroom until vouched for by a representative of one's unit. The adjutant could get quite touchy over these matters, and it would never do to be caught out twice. I have heard such responses as 'Catering Adviser to the Chinese Legation', etc., etc., given to a frustrated sentry. On one occasion, a sentry challenged approaching, if not steady footsteps with the usual 'Halt, who goes there?' The reply came back 'One drunken b . . . ' to which the sentry replied 'Advance you drunken b . . . . and be recognised.'

However there was little time for recreation or levity in late 1940 and 1941. Some relief was offered by the Royal Navy who kindly offered to take coast artillery officers on the minesweepers and motor torpedo boats, doing normal routine sweeps. A very close liaison and friendship had been built up between the R.N. unit officers, the minesweeper skippers, and the C.A. They visited our messes on the Eastern Arm and on the Pier Turret very frequently, and sometimes the more senior ranks visited the corps commander C.A. mess in Dover Castle, which in fact was situated next to the Vice Admiral Dover's headquarters, behind Cliff Block and facing the sea.

Two naval establishments in Dover were very helpful and co-operative:

H.M.S. Wasp, who controlled the M.G.B.'s and M.T.B.'s and air sea rescue craft, and *H.M.S. Lynx* in Dover College looked after administration. I was fortunate enough to have a trip on the minesweepers, on more than one occasion, right up to the Goodwin Sands off Deal and westward towards Dungeness. The trips on the M.T.B.'s and air sea rescue craft were, perhaps, even more exciting. The motor torpedo boat would approach the French cliffs at very high speed, to within a few miles. We could easily see the great German batteries, with their sentries and lookouts, peering down on us, but they did not open fire, as we presented an almost impossible target. Our danger lay only in attack by aircraft, and a vigilant watch was always kept in the sky. However it was hardly worth risking a valuable airplane to attack

A barrage balloon being taken out to a dumb barge to protect the harbour entrance.

121

one high speed boat, and so the Germans did not call one out. It might have been different if we had been spotted whilst they were returning from a raid. The air sea rescue vessels were clearly marked, and their task was to patrol the channel, especially after dog fights over the channel, or after some of our planes had been on raids on the channel ports. Fallen airmen of all nationalities were picked up. In addition, there was anchored in a line about five miles apart, and about seven miles out to sea, a chain of large buoyed shaped tanks. They contained survival kit, blankets and bunks, and were fixed with a small mast, so that the airman, or whoever managed to reach them, could indicate his presence. They were visited once a day by our own air sea rescue craft and also by German E-boats and rescue craft. They provided additional rescue facilities to anyone who could reach them. If the wrong nationality visited the buoy, the occupant was just unlucky and became a prisoner of war. Somehow or other, perhaps by mutual consent, British and German craft never visited the buoys at the same time and there was never any confrontation. Aircraft, likewise, always respected the rescue craft, and never attacked them, unless they considered they were engaged in a hostile act, such as photographing.

However there happened an incident which flagrantly contradicted this tacit understanding. It took place early in 1942, when I was the fire commander on duty in the F.C. post, Dover Castle. It was on a clear Sunday afternoon at about 14.30 hours. We sighted a small craft slowly approaching the port across the channel. The X.D.O. (Extended Defence Officer, R.N.) identified it as a German air sea rescue craft. As the range closed, I alerted the harbour batteries and advised the duty commander in the C.A. operations room, requesting instructions. He ordered me not to fire at the vessel unless I considered it had committed an hostile act, or was photographing our defences. The range closed to about 5000 yards and the vessel and her crew could be seen quite distinctly. I had all the guns round the harbour covering her and it was my decision. She could be sunk with the first salvo. However, beyond coming in very slowly, she appeared to be conducting herself properly and we concluded she might be looking for some German airman, who had been reported as shot down in the channel. In the circumstances, therefore, blowing her out of the water could hardly be justified. She seemed quite peaceful in her intentions, and after a short while she turned westward down the coast towards Dungeness, and we warned the

Battery commander and administration staff outside the officers' mess at Dover Castle in April 1942.

Motor gun boats
being prepared for
action in the
harbour.
An air sea rescue
vessel picking up a
British airman from
a rescue buoy.
Air Sea Rescue
insignia.

emergency batteries accordingly. One of our own air sea rescue craft was lying in the bay eastward of Dungeness. However, shortly before the German craft reached Littlestone, two Messerschmitts flew over from the landwards side, and dived upon the British craft, opening fire with their machine-guns. Of course it is just possible that they had mistaken her for an M.T.B., but they certainly did not stop and look at the clear identifying markings. She was soon blazing from stem to stern and sinking raidly. In a few moments, the German rescue craft had gone alongside to recue any survivors. There was nothing our shore batteries could do, and to open fire on the German vessel would only endanger the lives of the British seamen, if any, who had been picked up. The Royal Navy immediately ordered two fast M.T.B.'s out of Dover to intercept her, but she made straight back to Boulogne at full speed, and had too great a start to be stopped. Our own port war signal station did signal her and ask for the names of any survivors, and she answered giving the names of three men, one of whom was injured, and all were now prisoners of war.

German naval prisoners, captured at sea during the dog fights between our own craft and German E-boats in the channel, were frequently landed at Dover, and whereas the gunners were sometimes asked to provide escorts, we were never allowed to speak to the prisoners, as the intelligence corps insisted that they were better trained for such duties and would get more out of the prisoners. I noticed that on one occasion, when a number of prisoners were brought up to the Castle, some of the young seamen were no more than boys, looking very bewildered and frightened. One was openly crying, and I was informed later that the young seaman had explained that he had arranged to meet his fiancée in Boulogne that afternoon at 3 p.m. when he came off patrol. I think he expected us to let him keep the appointment, but in fact it was to be some years before he saw her again.

On glancing through the log book of Langdon Battery, I see that a number of very interesting persons and V.I.P.'s visited the fort.

11th July, 1941
    Battery inspected by Corps Commander 12th Corps (Lt. General B. L. Montgomery). Two series of 16 rounds fired from M.1 and M.2 guns. Very good shoot.
15th July
    Battery inspected by Sir John Dill, C.I.G.S.
5th September
    Battery inspected by Prime Minister of Canada, Rt. Hon. Mackenzie King, P.C.
3rd December
    Cat of doubtful lineage used B.O.P as a maternity ward to present battery with six healthy kittens.
13th April, 1942
    Visit to battery of H.E. The American Ambassador, Mr. J. Winant, the Army Commander, the Corps Commander (Lt. General B. Montgomery), Vice Admiral Dover, Admiral Sir B. H.

Three-inch anti-aircraft battery on the sea front at Dover, showing the range finder, predictor and spotter positions.

Ramsay, and Corps Commander Coast Artillery, Brigadier C. W. Raw. Concentration fire demonstration. One series of auto sight, 10 rounds fired per gun. 16 hits recorded. Warm praise from spectators!

(It was on this occasion that, just as we were ready to open fire, the naval minesweeping flotilla left harbour, on normal routine sweep, but fouling our range. The Vice Admiral expressed severe annoyance, as there would obviously be some delay before firing could commence, and especially in front of such distinguished visitors. He was embarrassed as the high ranking officers looked at him in amusement as the navy was the cause of the upset. The Admiral immediately sent a signal through the port war signal station, recalling all the vessels to harbour, and informing them that in no circumstances must they foul the gunners' range. This was the only occasion I can recall of the navy actually getting out of our way, to enable us to carry out our practice seawards.)

13th July
    Visit by Adjutant General.
There are a number of entries in the log book referring to other events, and administration, far too numerous to be quoted in full. A few are given by way of interest.

13th August
    70 rounds of enemy shell fire fell in battery vicinity. No serious casualties. Some damage.

16th August
    One round fired at 2100 hours at hostile plot. Range 10,850 yards. Target went out of range.
    16 rounds fired from French coast between 2100 and 2135 hours. One salvo in battery vicinity. No damage or casualties.
    2130. Gunfire heard in channel. Engagement between small naval craft.

18th August
    Alarm sounded at 0030 hours. Hostile plots at ranges 3000 yards to 6000 yards. Believed to be R-boats minelaying. Not engaged as navy taking action.

29th October
    Inspection by Brigadier Marshall, B.R.A.

11th November
    2349 hours. Enemy shelling. 6 rounds in Fan Bay area and 4 rounds in Harbour.

23rd November
    Inspection by General Paget.

10th December
    Continuous enemy shelling. 28 rounds in battery vicinity. Ceased 0045 hour.

11th December
    Enemy shelling. 20 rounds in battery area from bearings 160 to 120 degrees. Ceased 0145 hours.

18th January, 1943

2000 hours. Enemy aircraft attacked Dover with incendiary and H.E. bombs. Battery also attacked and stick of bombs fell across area as follows: —

Two 50 kg H.E. bombs between M.2 and M.3 emplacements. Concrete parapet wrecked and damage to four huts by flying concrete. Roof of war shelter cracked but no penetration.

One 50 kg H.E. bomb through roof and floor of No. 1 hut and burst outside. Hut damaged but saved by blast wall.

One 50 kg H.E. bomb through roof and floor of No. 7 hut causing damage by fire.

1 explosive incendiary at foot of 6 inch B.O.P. causing only small amount of damage. Two 50 kg fell near E water tank and failed to explode. No damage.

There was no damage to fighting efficiency of battery as a result of this attack. Some casualties in personnel.

8th February

Enemy aircraft dropped mines in harbour approaches and in front of Breakwater Battery. One aircraft crashed in western entrance.

10th February

Enemy shelling at convoy. About 50 rounds in battery area. Shelling ceased at 2125 hours.

During 1942/3 and later, there are almost daily entries in the log referring to bombs and shells in the area and on the town. Reference is also made to times and dates of our own counter bombardment and engagement of enemy shipping.

23rd June

Two Bofors guns installed in battery and manned by battery personnel.

21st September

Inspection by new B.R.A. S.E. Command, Brigadier E. B. de Foublanque.

4th January, 1944

Major B. E. Arnold assumed command of the battery on the transfer from the fire command, Dover Castle.

3rd May

Visit by Brigadier C. W. Raw, Corps Commander, Coast Artillery, accompanied by Colonel Schnieder, United States Air Force and other R.A.F. and U.S.A. Airforce officers.

5th June

Numerous convoys of all types passing through straits, westbound, including large hospital ship.

(The harbour at this time contained a number of dummy landing craft, made only of canvas and constructed in a prohibited area behind large screens, behind Waterloo Crescent on the seafront. Roads leading into the town contained obvious signs of preparation and facilities to accommodate long convoys of trucks, adding to the German belief that Dover would be the main port of assembly for the invasion of the continent.)

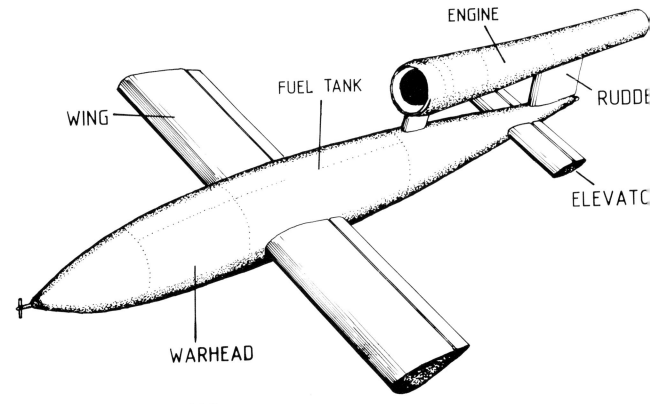

ENGINE

FUEL TANK

WING

RUDDE

ELEVATC

WARHEAD

6th June

0800 hours. German disclosure of first landings on French coast in Seine area, airborne and landing craft being used.

1145 hours. Convoy of 10 transports passed battery westward bound and engaged by enemy batteries. One large transport resembling a Liberty ship hit and number of explosions on board, followed by fire. Reported large number of casualties and survivors landed at Dover. Remainder of convoy protected by smoke screen by escorting vessels.

1746 hours. Transport vessel hit at 1205 hours, sank on bearing 085.30 degrees, still on fire.

7th June

1031 hours. Enemy engaged 28 transports passing westward. Escorting destroyers laid smoke screen. No serious damage reported.

7th June

1140 hours. Enemy fired 43 rounds at 8 large transports. Smoke screen by escorts and no serious damage.

15th June

2330 hours. Radio controlled plane or flying torpedo sighted, approaching from French coast.

(This was the first record in the battery of the opening offensive of the V1.)

2350 hours. Several more flying torpedos sighted, some passing over the battery. Fire Commander ordered Bofors to engage. Anti-aircraft fire over the town heavy. No hits recorded. Height of

The V-1 flying bomb, otherwise known as the doodlebug, was the first operational guided missile. It was designed to fly at 350 m.p.h. at an altitude of 3500 feet with a maximum range of 130 miles.

objects about 2000 feet. Planes show bright light at rear, believed to be a rocket attachment.

16th June

0007 hours. Engaged a number of flying bombs. No hits.

0014 hours. Flying bomb engaged and destroyed by A.A. fire west of battery. Nine flying bombs have so far been sighted passing overhead.

0120 hours. Bofors fired 98 rounds at 15 radio controlled planes passing over coast.

24th June

1430 hours. Enemy batteries engaging convoy. One vessel hit and beached between Dover and Folkestone. 21 rounds fell in harbour area.

26th July

Six gun enemy salvo straddled the Trinity House pilot cutter. (Four minus two plus.) Vessel appeared to be undamaged.

27th July

0001 hours. Alarm sounded. Battery brought to immediate readiness. Naval engagement in channel. Gunfire heard and tracers seen.

0300 hours. Normal routine resumed.

16th August

Flying bomb crashed at the base of the cliff, directly below B.O.P. Blast smashed door and other slight damage. No injury to personnel.

1st September

Heavy shelling in Dover, Folkestone and Deal areas. One round fell

The static 3·7 inch heavy anti-aircraft battery on the heights to the west of Dover at Farthingloe.

129

20 yards in front of No. 1 gun. Damage to billets. No casualties.
2nd September

Considerable naval activity in channel, mainly by light craft.
3rd September

1248 hours. Salvo of four shells, one on emergency B.O.P. Damage to surrounding buildings. No. 1 hut destroyed. Two wounded.

1310 hours. Large fire observed (probably oil) 2 degrees west of Calais Church.

1417 hours. Enemy now firing air bursts as well as H.E. between Dover and South Foreland. 52 rounds observed.
26th September

0200 to 0249. 0950 to 1343. Intermittent shelling from enemy guns on town and harbour.
26th September

1917 hours. Last round to be fired by German gunners fell in Castle Street. Information received on the 30th September that all enemy batteries had been overrun.

The log book gives many more and varied details throughout its length, but the above is an example of the type of entries, recorded almost daily by the duty officer in the battery observation post, Langdon Battery. All the other batteries recorded similar details and times when our own defences replied. These are recorded later.

There were many other activities in the battery, not recorded in the war diary. One was the excavation of a very old cannon of the Napoleonic era. It was sunk into the ground and only about three feet of the muzzle was visible. It had probably been used as a holdfast, when guns in the Langdon Battery had been installed. This old piece required a considerable amount of spade work round it, and in spite of the combined efforts of about three-quarters of the battery on ropes, it failed to come out of the ground. The captain quartermaster, hearing of our efforts, suggested powerful hydraulic jacks, and in fact, lent them to us. By this means, the old barrel was finally lifted. We cleaned it carefully and thoroughly and interesting crests and markings were revealed, although they were meaningless to us. It was probably an 18 pounder and our 'Tiffy' made us a wooden carriage for it, even with wheels. We mounted it with due ceremony at the entrance to the battery, alongside the guardroom, and a round was fired by inserting a thunderflash down the muzzle which discharged a small wooden ball quite a distance.

The visitors who inspected Langdon and the other forts were usually lunched and housed in the R.A. Fixed Defences Mess in Dover Castle, which was in fact the headquarters mess of the C.A. Operations Room, Corps Commander C.A. and regimental mess of the 519 Coast Regiment. The War Office usually set a standard of entertainment according to the importance of the visitors. The more important they were, so the monetary allowance was increased, and so we had a better lunch. We, in common with all units had at least two meatless days a week, more than our share of pilchards, dehydrated meat and vegetables, etc., but never to foreign visitors. The War Office also decided what the visitors should be allowed to see of the defences. Senior

Two of Dover's famous wartime visitors, Prime Minister Winston Churchill with the South African leader, Field Marshal Smuts. Several of Dover's citizens are recognisable including the mayor (Alderman J. Cairns), Labour party leader Councillor A. T. Goodfellow next to Chief Constable Saddleton, and Mr. Arthur Hobbs from the Town Clerk's department, second from left.

American Officers were usually granted a 'carte blanche' pass to all the defences, including radar, whilst others were only permitted to pass into the F.C. post or visit a harbour battery. Some were not always afforded this privilege even, and were then given a conducted tour of the historical features of Dover Castle, by a bombardier, well versed in the subject, who after the war became one of the official guides. The visitors must have been bored stiff, as ancient British history could have been of little interest to them, but that was not our problem. The greatest attraction in the later stages was a visit to the great cross-channel guns, at South Foreland and Wanstone.

When I was fire commander of the Harbour Command, and resided in the headquarters mess, we had on one occasion a visit by at least 15 high ranking Chinese officers, who spoke not a word of English. They were accompanied by the Chinese Ambassador, who acted as interpreter. They were a very jolly crowd and were not particularly interested in visiting anywhere, but contented themselves by remaining in the mess all the afternoon drinking. No real conversation could be carried out with them, but they were laughing and gesticulating all the time. Some of our junior officers could be seen singing and dancing around the mess, with their arms on the shoulders of a full Chinese general or admiral. The ambassador seemed rather amused by it all and registered

no complaint. They had enjoyed themselves too much. They were eventually poured into the official cars and, quite frankly, we were not too sorry to see them go.

We had visits from important personages from East and West Africa, and numerous visits from Emirs, Princes, Sultans and high ranking officers from Middle East countries; they always seemed to be dressed in their own traditional dress or uniform. Whilst we always provided an excellent meal, in accordance with the diet dictated by War Office, the gentlemen from the Middle East would take no alcohol, and a mess orderly was detailed to pick, most carefully, all the hairs off the chairs and cushions, these came from the mess dog 'Punch', a dalmatian, who was imprisoned upstairs until all the visitors had left. Nobody drank anything but water.

Such visits always meant a general clean-up in the batteries, with plenty of whitewash to bring them up to inspection order. The white lines at the rear of the guns were freshened up, and in spite of some grumbling, every effort was made to impress the visitor. This inspired one battery commander to produce an instrument resembling a long thermometer, set in an elaborate wooden casing, and displayed at the entrance to the battery. Across it he had painted the word 'Oxometer', and when asked to explain its meaning and use, he would reply, 'An instrument to measure the amount of 'bull' required before a visit by a V.I.P.'.

The batteries in general fared no better or worse than the headquarters mess, except on special occasions. It was always being remarked that if enough water was added to the dehydrated meat, it would eventually turn back into the original cow. Sometimes we had pilchards for breakfast, pilchards for dinner and plenty left over for tea, if we could face them. They seemed to be the staple diet, and certainly appeared on the menu three or four times a week if not more. The cooks bravely tried to conceal them. They fried them in bread crumbs, they boiled them, they disguised them in batter and bread crumbs, but whatever they did, the good old pilchard always won in the end. Perhaps the cruellest cut of all was on one occasion, when I was granted 48 hours leave, I travelled up to my temporary home in Hollingbourne. My wife, to my horror, had expended precious point coupons from her ration book to buy me a tin of pilchards for my tea, as a treat.

At Christmas time, especially later in the war, when rationing became less difficult, the cooks usually excelled themselves in producing an excellent Christmas dinner. At Christmas time, the officers served the food and waited at table. This was a custom dating back many years, and as far as possible, was always observed. An excellent spirit always prevailed, with a lot of good humoured leg pulling. The lowest rank in the battery, the sanitary orderly's mate, always insisted on buying the battery commander a beer, and a good time was had by all, except the watch on duty. We felt the sort of trick the Germans might play would be to make a raid on Christmas Day. It was also customary at Christmas time for the commanding officer, accompanied by the fire commander and the R.S.M., to visit all the batteries in his command, and by the time we reached the Castle at the end of our journey, we were feeling slightly the worse for wear. Similar parties were held in the other batteries, and on Pier Turret usually the minesweeper officers and their crews would join in, and the battery received a similar invitation from the minesweepers to a party on board. The vice admiral invited the officers of the R.A. Fixed Defences, who only lived next door, to lunch time drinks, and sadly on one occasion, instigated I believe by the admiral's flag officer, a game of rugby suddenly developed with somebody's hat, and the admiral and corps commander retreated diplomatically to quieter quarters.

Another recollection of life in a coast battery was impressed upon my mind during my tour of duty as battery commander of Langdon. On Sundays, we occasionally had a visit from the local padre, who conducted a short service in the barrack room huts, behind the guns. As he had many such visits to make to other batteries and anti-aircraft sites, his visits to Langdon could not be more than one in three Sundays. However I felt that it was my job to see that these Sunday services should not suffer, because the padre was unable to visit us, and so I announced that, though unqualified in more ways than one, I would conduct the service myself. I had a Holy Bible and Common Prayer Book and so I selected one or two well known hymns, which the battery clerk typed out in the form of hymn sheets. The order of service was merely one or two prayers, a reading from the bible and a couple of hymns, usually the same ones every Sunday. There was certainly no sermon and the lesson was picked at random. Such services were voluntary, but surprisingly were usually well attended. I am not sure that the word voluntary applied, as far as the battery sergeant major was concerned. I know he took little notice of religious persuasion, and Jews, R.C.'s and Church of England were all the same to him. A parade was a parade, even if the B.C. had said it was voluntary. Perhaps it was a break in the monotony that persuaded the men to attend, I cannot believe that it was for the good of their souls. My choice of hymns had obviously to be hymns and tunes well known to the men. If we had the service in the canteen, there was an old piano which could provide music, if we could find a pianist, otherwise we sang without accompaniment. It always struck me as rather poignant that a hymn I selected, No. 165 A & M ('O God our help in ages past'), and sung with great gusto, contained a verse I felt particularly appropriate, as I surveyed my congregation, many of whom had been on duty that night, and now looking a little weary, and looking forward to bed, when the hut had been cleared. The verse was as follows: —

> A thousand ages in Thy sight,
>   Are like an evening gone,
> Short as the watch that ends the night,
>   Before the rising sun.

Many of the gunners who had just come off duty did not consider the watch to have been all that short, and all had certainly witnessed the rising sun.

And so life drifted on. Many of the original territorials had now departed. Two batteries had been exchanged with the Orkneys. Some officers had gone into civil affairs, and many of the younger officers and men transferred into other units and Field Artillery. Most of the officers had been sent on a variety of courses: Physical Training and Messing at Aldershot, Transport at Tonbridge, Advance Field Tactics at Tunbridge Wells. A shop in the Pantiles had been converted for this purpose and we were billeted out in private houses in the town. The School of Gunnery was transferred from Shoeburyness to a safer area at Llandudno in North Wales, and every officer attended on one course or another, usually more than once. The Hotel Gogarth Abbey, at the end of the Great Orme, was used as billets, mess and class rooms.

We had senior Canadian officers attached to us at Dover for experience, and they were either posted to a battery, or lived in the R.H.Q. mess in the Castle. We also sent officers to Canada, to train them on many new equipments, then being installed in that country, and even a series of lectures in the U.S.A. In my own case, I was posted to Victoria, B.C., then to Prince Rupert in Northern British Columbia, and even as far as Ketchikan in Alaska, attached to an American unit, but that is another story.

We undertook many other duties, in addition to our battery tasks: regimental security officer, military liaison officer, whose duty it was to form a close liaison with the chief air raid warden in Dover. In the event of a heavy raid, and all the town's services being destroyed, arrangements were made for emergency services and communications to be taken over by the military as well as police duties. In point of fact, it never became necessary for this operation to be put into effect, but persons were detailed to stand by, should it happen, as in the case of the blitz on Canterbury.

It might be worth mentioning at this juncture that, when I was attached to 109 Coast Battery, Royal Canadian Artillery, Esquilmalt, B.C. and later 5th Northern B.C. Coast Regt. R.C.A., I had with me a number of pieces of chalk which I had removed from the cliffs at Langdon. A local gunner in the Castle had carved a dozen or so pieces into ashtrays, etc. and painted on the side that they had come from the Dover Cliffs. I took them with me to Canada, and they caused me some embarrassment, as they were in heavy demand both from the Americans and the Canadians, and it became difficult for me to allocate them without giving offence and disappointment. I wonder if any still exist.

Another rather pleasant contact was established with an American whilst I was still stationed in Dover. We had been receiving a number of parcels of comforts such as socks, pullovers, and balaclava helmets, knitted by generous ladies' societies, such as the British War Relief, and these were distributed to the batteries. Whilst unpacking such a parcel in the fire command post, I came across a short note, attached to a balaclava helmet. It was inscribed 'Knitted by Mrs. Nutter, British War Relief Society, Springfield, India Orchard, U.S.A.' I thought it would be rather nice to write and thank this good lady, so one night whilst on duty, I composed a suitable letter, saying how much the troops appreciated the efforts of the American ladies and herself. I then waxed rather sentimental in as much as I informed her that whilst we waited for Jerry on the cold bleak cliffs of Dover, and only 20 miles away from him, we were greatly heartened by our good friends overseas, etc., etc. For some reason I imagined that this was the sort of stuff the American ladies would like to read, even supposing my letter reached them.

To my astonishment, a few weeks later, I received a long letter from Mrs. Nutter, stating that this was the first acknowledgment received by them, direct from the recipient. She was absolutely elated and the story appeared in the American press, under the title, 'English Coast Artilleryman writes to Mrs. Nutter'. They then went on to print my letter in full, which I found rather touching. At least I felt it had helped to improve the relationship between the U.S.A. and ourselves, especially as the U.S.A. had not yet entered the war. I was even more pleased when a very large box of American candies was delivered to the fire command post, the type forwarded to American forces overseas.

Another, less pleasant duty, allocated to officers, usually attached to R.H.Q., was attendance at Field General Courts Martial, firstly as members, then as defending officer, and later as President. Sometimes, if the case was complicated, we had the benefit of advice from a member of the Judge Advocate's department, but mostly it was a case of desertion or absence without leave. I used to find the task very distasteful, but it had to be done. When on a course at Aldershot, I was looking through the windows of Gale and Polden Ltd., and there saw a little book entitled 'Vade Mecum for Field General Courts Martial'. I purchased the book for only a few coppers and found it to be extremely useful as a guide. I was aware that these military trials were conducted in the fairest possible manner. Every opportunity to defend himself and every assistance was always afforded the prisoner, and he was always given the benefit of the doubt. One extremely difficult case arose and was tried in Dover Castle. Although I attended, it was not in any official capacity, except as a witness. This concerned a gunner on the Eastern Arm, who one day refused to go on duty, or even put on his battledress. The B.S.M. gave him a direct order to go on watch and when he refused, he sent for me. I could do no more and order him to go on duty and again he refused. He then informed me that he was 21 years old that day. He asserted that according to international law, he was entitled to elect his nationality. Although he had been born and brought up in England, and in fact his mother, was English, his father was Italian, and all his living relatives were Italian. Accordingly he now elected to become an Italian citizen and as we were now at war with Italy, he was an enemy. He stated that he did not wish to be placed in a position whereby he would be called upon to fight his cousins. This was of course far and away above me, but I could still charge him with disobeying a lawful command, whatever his reasons. As he still refused to do so, there was nothing left that could be done but put him in the guard room and advise R.H.Q. He remained there for two or three days, playing cards with the guards and everyone seemed to think the whole business rather amusing. He was eventually taken up to the Castle and as nobody knew anything about international law, a civilian solicitor was employed to prepare his case. The trial lasted some time and his plea was accepted that it would not be fair to order

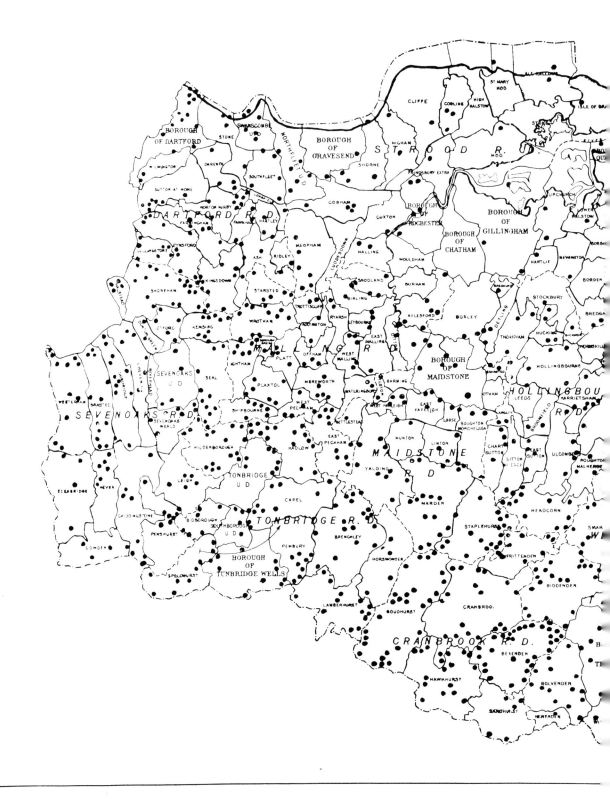

Where the Doodle Bugs Crashed in K

Reproduced by kind permission of the 'Kent Messenger'.

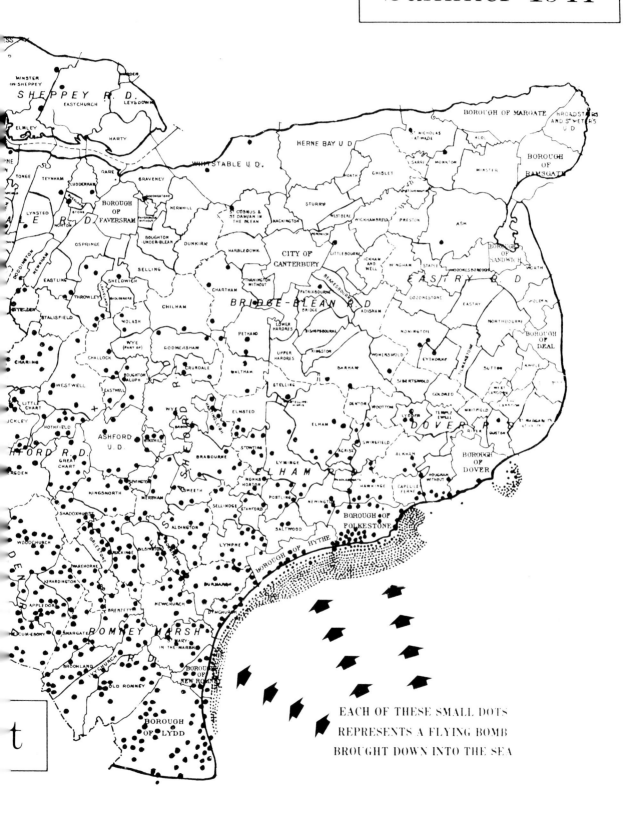

Summer 1944

EACH OF THESE SMALL DOTS
REPRESENTS A FLYING BOMB
BROUGHT DOWN INTO THE SEA

him to fight his own relatives. He was discharged from the army and placed in a labour camp. I never saw him again, but I was sorry as on occasions, he had stood in for the cook, and proved to be an excellent worker; no doubt due to his civilian calling.

Another pastime thought up by our masters was an exercise in the art of 'Gun bucking', or to give it the correct title, 'The Principles of Moving Ordnance'. The idea was to bring up a six inch gun on rollers, and raise it up a bank, about 30 feet high, and fire it, all in one day. The purpose of the exercise was to try out the installation of a coast gun in a captured enemy port, either in Northern France or Belgium or Italy. We had not captured any of these ports yet, but it was considered that should ever the time come, it would be as well to know how to protect them from sea attack.

Langdon Barracks was chosen as the most suitable place, being on more than one level, and approximately the correct heights. In addition, all the skidding, such as planks, 10 foot, 6 foot, and 4 foot, oak and fir, blocks, rollers, holdfasts, ropes and shackles, were in fact stored in Langdon, and readily available. The exercise was not to be performed by experts in gun installation, who in the event would probably not be available, but was to be done by an ordinary gunner officer from 519 Coast Regiment. As many men as could be spared from the batteries would be detailed to assist him. Any notes he had made on courses, any knowledge or advice he could squeeze out of professional gun buckers, plus Coast Artillery Training Part II, the manual devoted to such things, would be at his disposal. The only concessions given were the laying down of a concrete base, with the required number of bolts, on which to set the carriage down and fix, when it had been raised up to the second level. This was cheating, I thought, as it was unlikely the enemy would be so obliging. The other concession was the bringing of the whole piece to the entrance of Langdon Barracks, by the experts. The holding down bolts in the concrete base are still there today, and likely to remain there for all time. A number of senior officers from other regiments, from Brigade headquarters, including the B.R.A. and other 'brass hats' and the corps commander C.A. would be invited to witness the event or catastrophe, as we all expected it to be, and all of us wondered who the unfortunate officer, to be detailed by the Commanding officer, would be. Obviously the exercise could not be rehearsed beforehand, and everybody was hoping they would be spared the trials and tribulations which would surely follow.

Her Majesty Queen Elizabeth visiting a warden's post somewhere in Dover in November 1944, little thinking that she would return thirty-five years later as Lord Warden of the Cinque Ports and Constable of Dover Castle.

We patiently awaited regimental orders and finally to everyone else's relief, the name appeared, it was mine! My knowledge for such a task was extremely limited, but the C.O. was very enthusiastic and gave me every possible assistance and advice. We selected from the regiment, about 50 men and many had actually served in a regiment trained for the installation of guns. I closeted myself, however, with the greatest expert of all, who happened to be in Dover at the time. This man had recently put new barrels into Citadel Battery and was responsible for the installation of the great guns at South Foreland, Wanstone, and Fan Bay. He had in fact, put guns into fortifications all over the world, and

WARDENS POST Z4

POLICE NOTICE

FULL BLACK OUT
RESTRICTIONS
ARE
STILL IN FORCE
IN THIS DISTRICT

knew more about such matters, I suspect, than any other gunner living. He was rather an irascible and fierce looking man, with a dark tanned complexion of India, and a liking for gin. This was the great Major later Lt. Colonel 'Dickie' Shrive. He was always followed about by the most enormous battery sergeant major I have ever seen, and certainly with the loudest voice and 'powers of persuasion'. This man was called 'Tiny'. Dickie Shrive virtually trained me on all I wanted to know, what to do and what equipment I should require. He explained all the principles of moving ordnance, and the things in C.A.T. Vol. II, which I did not understand. He stressed that at all times I should never forsake safety to speed up the job or take a short cut. He explained that I should require a 12 ton gin for lifting. This consisted of a very large tripod, which had to be erected with a barrel and tackle, strong enough to lift a six inch gun on to a constructed sledge. The erection of the gin was a drill in itself. Its legs had to be inserted into 'shoes' to prevent them sinking into the ground, and it had to be equally balanced on its three legs, so that it did not collapse under stress, and crash down on the people operating it. It had the advantage, however, inasmuch as it was something on which we could practise and rehearse up at Langdon Barracks, until we were more or less competent to put the thing up, in the least possible time and difficulty. This job was in addition to my normal duties as fire commander, but we were given about two months to get ready and the C.O. was very good about letting me have as much time off as possible for my 'gin' work and other preparations. I now had to make all the calculations for ultimate strength, safe working strength, stress and breaking stress, for timber and ropes. I had to learn about 14 foot levers and power required to balance fulcra and a host of other information which I should probably never require again. We then drew up plans and read all about the building of ramps, for it was by such a contraption the gun was to be hauled up the bank. Many of these things I worked out and read up during the night watches, enemy permitting. This plan I have kept as a memento to the very anxious and worrying time I experienced prior to the exercise. However I received every encouragement from Major Shrive, and he looked over my calculations to ensure that I had not made a fool of myself and that nobody was going to get hurt, because I had ordered the wrong plank in the wrong place!

When the great day arrived, there was little more for me to do, other than issue the necessary orders and pray everything would go according to plan and that we had made the right calculations. Fortunately it was a fine bright day, and the gun and carriage had arrived safely at the entrance of the barracks. All the V.I.P.'s started to arrive and chairs had been placed for them at the higher level, and an officer was there to explain to them our intention. Even a six inch shell was placed ready to be fired, if ever we got that far.

The men got to work to build the ramp up the bank, quickly and efficiently, and I am sure many of them had done the job before. Next we erected the gin without mishap, and I thought all this is too good to be true. All through the morning, cars kept arriving in Langdon Barracks, to take up position in the army way, according to rank, to witness the rise of the gun and carriage to its concrete base or fall on the officer responsible for its journey. We hammered in the holdfasts with great flourish, to impress the visitors, raised the carriage high enough to place rollers under the sledge, to enable us to drag it to the foot of the ramp. This in itself was a mathematical calculation, based on the diameter of the rollers and the width of the bottom of the sledge. It would be determined when a roller would reach the end of the sledge and when another must be inserted in the front, so that the movement forward went off smoothly and without tilting the carriage. If the rollers were placed at an angle, so the sledge moved left or right. We got it to the foot of the ramp and attached a number of ropes, blocks and tackle fastening the end to the holdfasts at the higher level. I placed a couple of men with mallets alongside the holdfasts, in case they started to drag out of the ground, and it proved just as well, as I learnt afterwards. The gods were with us that day, for somehow, no doubt due to the resourcefulness of the sergeant in charge and the co-operation and enthusiasm of the men, the carriage reached the top, was again placed on rollers, and finally lowered on to the bolts in the concrete base, where it was securely fixed by men detailed just for this job.

After adjustment to our sledge, the barrel followed, and started its hazardous journey up the ramp. The operation is known as parbuckling, which simply means that ropes are rolled round the barrel in such a way that it can be virtually rolled up the ramp. The men following behind had a dangerous job, as they were required to put triangular shaped blocks, called scotches, against the barrel, to prevent it rolling backwards. If it had done so, I doubt whether they could have stopped it, and would have been badly injured, and this was quite contrary to what Major Shrive had taught me. It was a case of the drill being forgotten or not enough confidence in the theory. All I had to do was stand at the top, directing the operation, yell 'heave' on a number of occasions, and shout encouragement. I think I even took a turn on the rope, although this was considered 'not the thing', as I was not then in a position to watch the proceedings. I was supposed to be in charge, and know all that was going on. In fact, I was relying almost entirely on the skill and drive of the sergeant. Very slowly the barrel rolled up the ramp, with rather terrifying pauses as the men stopped to get their breath, the follow up men scotched up, and the holdfast men hammered at the holdfasts, which were creaking and appeared to be working loose. If they had given way, the barrel would have crashed to the bottom and a number of gunners would have been seriously injured. Finally it reached the top and now it was just a question of lowering the gin, getting it up the ramp and again raising it so that the barrel could be lifted and lowered on to the trunnions. Gin drill can be quite impressive to the uninitiated, and although hot and tired, you can be sure that everybody put in all the 'bull' they could to impress the onlookers, who by this time, had enjoyed their picnic lunches, and were now getting rather bored with the whole business, especially as we had provided no excitement, like a major accident. When the barrel was finally resting in the trunnion holders, we screwed down everything in sight, fixed on the breech and then my most important task became due. I proudly marched across to the corps commander and reported. 'Gun ready to load and fire.' We had the six inch sand filled shell, together with a charge, and although I could not see why, I felt that the whole thing would collapse, as in a funny film, if we attempted to fire it. Nevertheless, the corps commander inspected the piece, appeared to be satisfied, ordered me to load and make safe, which merely meant pulling back the lever breech mechanism a few inches so that contact was broken. He then ordered me to fire when ready, so the detachment, which had been well rehearsed, took up their positions, the gun was laid in the direction of France, for want of a better place to aim, I ordered 'Fire' and kept my fingers crossed. There was the usual explosion and all the loose grass and chalk rose in the air in a great cloud, part settling on the spectators, who had by now retired to a safe distance, and lo and behold, but a few seconds later, a great splash arose in the channel about 5000 yards away. This was followed by a little clapping from the spectators, who then hurried to their cars and disappeared. We had started the exercise at 8 a.m. and the time was now 1630 hours. Everyone was relieved, no more than I, the C.O. was delighted, as he would receive the congratulations from the corps commander, and the bored visitors had now all gone, thinking that the whole business had probably been a waste of their time and our efforts. Major Shrive, who had turned up late in the afternoon, so that he would not have to witness the fuss we were making over a job his own boys would have done in a quarter of the time, with half the number of men, made us all stack the skidding in a neat pile. All our planks, four by twos, ropes and tackle had to be laid out in an orderly manner, as his own unit would be round next morning to dismantle the equipment in a very short time and without any bother. Nevertheless, I shall be eternally grateful to this gruff and frightening man, for the help and advice he had given me. Without it, I have no doubt whatsoever, the whole business would have been a dismal failure.

However, gun shifting for me was not always so successful. I was ordered to put a Bofors gun on top of the turret of the six inch on Pier

519 Coast Regiment, Dover, football team in 1943/4.

Turret Battery. This was virtually on the iron roof, behind the guns. This large flat iron roof was in fact the cover of the old 81 tonners of yesteryear. When they were put in, I cannot imagine that anybody then imagined that some fifty years later, an anti-aircraft gun, would have to be mounted above them.

I assembled the men to build a ramp from the pier to the top of the turret, and felt that a Bofors being so much lighter than a six inch, my task would not be so formidable. Also there were no onlookers to criticise. The height I suppose was about 25 feet, just a little less than Langdon. The ramp went up easily enough, but now we were on concrete and iron and had nowhere to sink our holdfasts. We did the best we could, and all sorts of people came forward with suggestions, but none of them seemed to work. The gun was still sitting below on the pier and even the enemy had let off a few rounds, which fell nearby, and did little to give us confidence. By 1600 hours we had made no further progress, and we were still in the same position as we were at 1100 hours, when the ramp had been completed. I was in complete despair, and really did not know what to do next, except report back to the Castle that I had fallen down on the job. Then fate took a turn to help me. There appeared along the pier and on rails, one of those small cranes, used to load luggage on to cross channel boats in peacetime. A gentleman, wearing about two waistcoats, and smoking a short pipe, peered down at me through a small and rather dirty window. He said he had been watching my antics most of the day with some amusement and that now I had apparently been defeated, he enquired whether I would like his help. I would have accepted help from Hitler himself, if he had been there. Our friend directed how a few ropes should be fixed round the Bofors, lowered his crane and within seven minutes, my Bofors was settled nicely in position on top of the turret. I went over to the crane to thank my benefactor, but he was already moving off in his crane, chuckling to himself, and thinking what a lot of fools we were, and heaven help the country if it depended on our ingenuity. I am sure he could have come over much earlier, if he had wanted to, but preferred to see how we would get on first. I reported back to the colonel that the gun was now in position, but it was not until a long time afterwards, that I told him how it got there.

And so with our court martial, our gun shifting, our football, and our endless training, life went on through 1942, 1943, and into 1944. It became obvious to all that all threat of an invasion had now passed, but we had to remain prepared and ready for a parachute or commando attack on any of the batteries, or a raid on the harbour and its installations. We were now more heavily defended than at any time during the war and the success of any such raid became very doubtful. There were now fewer and fewer of the original Territorials. The first to leave had been the men posted to the 5th Super Heavy Regiment in 1940. Pier Turret Battery, with all its personnel, had been posted to the Orkneys, and they had been replaced by a battery of similar strength from those Islands. A new battery of two four inch guns had been set up on the Knuckle, and also manned by a battery posted down from the

Orkneys. The next posting of a considerable number of men from the three regiments 519, 540 and 520, to a new regiment being formed, the 203rd Fixed Defences. Our own commanding officer, Lt. Col. S. C. Tomlin, was given command of the new regiment, which was being posted to Italy to protect shipping in the captured Italian ports, which they did most successfully. In one engagement when 12 Italian midget submarines accompanied by five large motor torpedo boats, attacked our shipping at Leghorn, they were engaged with such vigour, that by next morning only one small vessel was still afloat and limping home to Genoa. He was quickly dispatched by the R.A.F., so that in all 17 vessels paid the price. It would not be entirely wrong to say that the result was in no small measure due to the Dover training they had received.

By mid 1944, it was decided that more men could be posted to more active service, and the local Home Guard, which consisted of a number of Dover Harbour employees, and commanded by the Harbour Superintendent, should be trained in the art of coast defence. They were instructed on the Pier Turret battery and conducted their own practice seawards with enthusiasm and success, so that it can rightly be written

The Prime Minister inspecting a guard of honour of Wrens drawn up on top of the submarine pens in Dover Harbour. Mrs. Churchill is behind the captain.

144

that the defence of the port and town of Dover was once more in the hands of its local townsfolk.

The final drain came with the formation of the 614 Regiment, R.A. This was a new regiment to be trained in infantry tactics, to take over the captured towns of Europe, to police them and carry out an infantry role. The original destination of 614 Regiment was Antwerp. The regiment formed up in tented quarters in Broome Park, a country estate a few miles outside Dover, on the road to Canterbury, and had infantry instructors posted to it. In January, in thick snow, it was moved to Bakehouse Camp, near Saltash in Cornwall, where with two other regiments it continued very vigorous infantry training and manoeuvres, including mine lifting and anti-tank roles. The destination had now been changed to the reoccupation of the Channel Islands, and the island allotted to the Dover regiment, 614, was Guernsey and later Alderney. The story of this venture has already been described in greater detail in 'The Alderney Story'.

Finally the batteries became no more than holding units. Large numbers of warrant officers and senior N.C.O.'s were posted in with no specific duties to perform. The state of readiness in the batteries was reduced finally by the end of 1944 and the beginning of 1945, by being placed in care and maintenance, which simply meant that they were no longer operational.

The regiments were no longer corps troops, but became part of the South Eastern Army, with a tiger's head replacing the three trees. Very few of the original volunteers remained with the exception of the older men or those of low medical category. It is however, worthy of mention and reported that the trained coast artillery men, whether they were posted to anti-tank, field or even infantry regiments, were greatly appreciated and admired by the units to which they were posted, because of their high state of training, discipline and experience.

After the war, the Territorial Army was again reformed and once again local volunteers, most of them now with war time experience in a variety of units, came forward to learn how to defend the town. The new volunteers came from the infantry, artillery, parachute regiments and commandos, and had been trained on a host of different weapons. They were now required to undergo training in the new coast artillery, with new methods based on wartime experience and advanced techniques. They now manned the six inch at Fan Bay, (Langdon had now been abandoned), Eastern Arm twin six, Southern Breakwater six inch and twin six, and the twelve pounders on the Pier Extension. The history and the forming of the new Dover regiment, 410 Coast Regiment, R.A.T.A. with its headquarters still in the old Liverpool Street Drill Hall, used by the volunteers of two world wars, and still retaining its old riding school, is however another story. The old volumes of Coast Artillery Training Part I no longer applied, and rules of ranging, such as the old system of ladder fire, passed into history.

12 Our reply

"Polish me well and keep me clean,
And I will put a ball on Calais green."
—*Unknown.*

We must now go back in time to learn something of the guns which were installed to meet the danger of invasion and to keep the channel clear of German shipping, in accordance with the orders issued by Mr. Churchill. The story has been unfolded of the states of readiness of the defenders to meet the threat of 1940-41, and their unpreparedness to meet the demands of modern warfare. I have also related some of the history of the great guns brought up by the Germans to bombard the seaside towns, to close the Strait to British and allied shipping, and to assist them in their invasion plans.

Slowly but surely counter weapons were brought into being, not just to defend Dover, but also provide answering fire to the German guns, but mainly to close the straits, and provide protection against an invading fleet, should the need arise. Unlike the Germans, however, the British guns were not to be used to bombard the French coast and seaside towns, and only at the end of the war, when the Canadians were approaching the German batteries, did they have a landwards role.

One of the railway guns with enthusiastic crew.

As has already been stated, the prime minister was most anxious that formidable defences by way of large calibre guns should be installed as soon as possible. Numerous minutes were directed to the C.I.G.S. with this end in view. Even at the expense of the navy, guns must be found in its stores, powerful enough, so that the Germans should not have it all their own way. The somewhat ineffectiveness of Winnie and Pooh, the fourteen inch guns, manned by the Royal Marine Siege Regiment, were a start. There followed, later, railway mounted artillery, Sceneshifter, Gladiator, Piecemaker, all mobile 13.5 inch mounted at Lydden, Martin Mill, and Guston Tunnel, respectively, and Bochebuster, an 18 inch howitzer at Bekesbourne, was manned by the R.A., but this gun never actually went into action.

If the Strait was to be closed, it was essential that modern coast artillery guns, with the latest type of range finding equipment and detection be provided. For this purpose, a new regiment along the cliffs to the east of the town, came into being. 540 Coast Regiment, R.A., commanded by Lt. Colonel J. H. W. G. Richards, a very experienced gunnery officer, and formerly commandant of a Coast Training Regiment. By February, 1941, Fan Bay Battery, with three 6 inch guns and a range of 25,000 yards was ready. This was shortly followed by South Foreland Battery, near St. Margaret's Bay, with four 9.2 guns and a range of 31,000 yards, operational by October, 1941. Finally the great Wanstone Battery of two 15 inch guns known as Clem and Jane, after the deputy prime minister, Mr. Clement Attlee and the young lady from the cartoon in the *Daily Mirror*, who was popular, by continually losing her clothes. Wanstone had a range of 42,000 yards and nearly 50,000 yards if super charged. The guns were operational by June, 1942. The swept channel, used by the Germans, closed to 26,000 yards, and so the German shipping was within range of both South Foreland and Wanstone from the time it left Boulogne to almost into Calais.

The regiment had its own fire command post, and the latest equipment and radar, rangefinding, fire direction tables, and everything as sophisticated and modern, as it was possible to devise for coast artillery. The operation rooms were set in concrete bunkers, underground, and protected from shell fire, except from a direct hit. The regiment was manned by officers of practical experience and training and by instructor gunners, and power for the batteries supplied by great engines, also well protected against bomb and shell splinters. The batteries also had large camouflaged nets and an officer, specially trained in setting up means of disguise, was attached to the regiment. No expense or effort was spared, to ensure that this regiment could in itself meet the demands of Mr. Churchill, and give a good account of itself against anything the Germans had to offer. It was operationally controlled by the C.A. operations room in the Castle casemates and a very close liaison with the Royal Navy was maintained. This liaison and working together of the services was soon to pay good dividends.

The German practice of sending small protected convoys through the straits was now stopped and a heavier burden was now placed on the already overworked French railway system. The Germans, like ourselves,

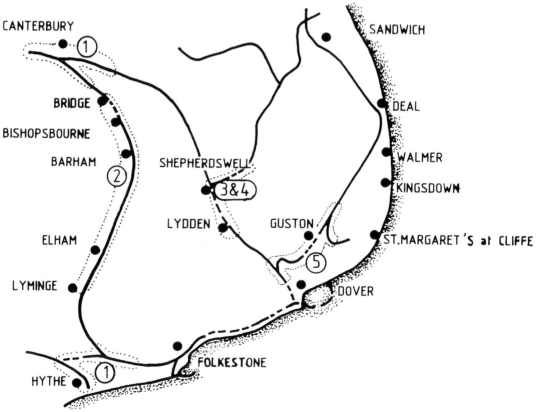

were obliged to keep their channel swept of mines twice a day on each tide, and round Cap Blanc Nez and Cap Gris Nez, they seemed particularly vulnerable to attack from our guns. The Germans were therefore forced to run fast single merchantmen, through the straits, with essential cargoes, at the darkest period of the month, when the tide was at its highest. Escorts and escorted even elected to keep close to the French cliffs and darkness gave them some protection from the British motor torpedo boats. However this was no deterrent to the new coast artillery. Vessels could now be picked up on radar, whilst still in Boulogne Harbour, and if they were still there in daylight, their presence confirmed by the R.A.F. air patrols, Jim Crow and Patrol Reconnaissance Unit. Many large merchant vessels carrying strategic war materials, such as iron ore, from Spain, had been using the Strait and their destruction was essential to the British war effort.

The C/D C.H.L. radar sets were fully operational by February, 1941, and available as a means of ranging for South Foreland and Wanstone. They were adequate for long distance firing, provided the target was of reasonable size, say 750 tons and over. They could also be used to detect fall of shot, being able to follow the line of the shell and pick up the splash when it fell into the sea. This conveyed vital information to the battery commander, conducting the shoot, as he could now order a correction to the guns, depending on whether the rounds had fallen left or right or plus or minus of the target. If the salvo fell within the target vicinity, so that the target echo on the radar corresponded with the target echo of the fall of shot, it was reasonable to record a hit. We had advanced a long way since our T.A. drill hall days, with our miniature range, the irate adjutant's pencil drumming on the desk, to represent fall of shot, and the range reports of a seasick range officer on the old *Sir Robert Whigham*. The system of ladder firing was now archaic in just a few years, and we now thought that we had reached the ultimate in the science of coast gunnery and the defence of the U.K. It never occurred to us that but fifteen years later, all coast artillery would become obsolete.

There were numerous engagements by the 6 inch batteries against E-boats and R-boats, who like our own M.T.B.'s were merely raiding parties, out to sink anything which happened to cross their path. A favourite trick was to leave one of their number tied up to a buoy, marking our swept channel. The echo of the buoy on our radar sets was known and would accordingly correspond with the echo of the enemy E-boat, so the latter's presence could not be detected. As soon as some merchantman, convoy, or even one of our own patrol boats passed by, then out would go the torpedoes, and the E-boat make with all possible speed for its home base, with a few six inch shells in its wake, with little likelihood of any hits.

It was on the 6th February, 1942, that Fan Bay Battery first went into action. On the orders of the corps commander C.A., from the Dover operations room, they were instructed to engage a number of E-boats, in mid channel, sailing westwards. The engagement lasted 20 minutes and although a number of rounds fell in the target area, the results were unknown nor any sinkings confirmed. It was not until 12th February,

Prime Minister Winston Churchill inspecting one of the railway guns in its firing position. Below—a map showing the position of the various railway guns. 1. 9·2 inch Mark 13, 2. Boche Buster 18 inch howitzer, 3 & 5. Gladiator 13·5 inch, Sceneshifter 13·5 inch, Piecemaker 13·5 inch, 4. 12 inch howitzers mark 3 & 5.

1942, that the first big engagement against enemy shipping took place. This was the occasion of the dash through the channel by the German capital ships, *Scharnhorst, Gneisenau* and *Prinz Eugen.* Early warning of their approach was given by the radar sets along the south coast, and although some of the old C.H.L. sets were jammed, the more modern range-finding radar and 12 cm sets were clear and on target. The South Foreland Battery had plenty of time to get ready and load and the shoot was to be conducted by the local fire commander on duty, who would receive his instructions from the C.A. operations room. The visibility had closed to about 5000 yards and the vessels therefore were not visible to the naked eye. As they reached Boulogne, the time was just before noon. The Germans provided an umbrella cover of Messerschmitts, a number of destroyers and escort vessels, so that when the six Swordfish aircraft from Manston, led by Lt. Commander Esmonds (posthumously awarded the V.C.) attacked with torpedoes and no escorting Spitfires or Hurricanes, they were virtually going straight into their deaths, with little hope of success in their mission. Although they pressed home their attack, their torpedoes failed to damage the enemy, and all six aircraft were brought down.

South Foreland (9.2) controlled by the fire commander, opened fire a few minutes before 12 noon, and 33 rounds of A.P.C. were fired over a period of 17 minutes, into the target area. The German long range guns immediately replied, supporting the passage of their ships, by a continuous bombardment of both the town and battery areas. The ships, to everybody's chagrin, continued their passage and were in fact too heavily armoured to be effectively damaged by the coast artillery guns. They had resisted constant heavy air attack at Brest and a 380 lb. 9.2

Improved radar allowed more accurate plotting of targets and accuracy of shelling.

shell was unlikely to impede their progress through the Strait. It is perhaps ironic that the great Wanstone Battery was not ready for action until the following August when quite a different story might have been told. However, when the corps commander attended the inevitable enquiry at the War Office, it was revealed that one of the Swordfish pilots had reported that he had observed three explosions on the deck of the *Prinz Eugen*, and as no bombs could be attributed to the British aircraft, three direct hits were credited to the Dover battery. There may well have been more, but at least three hits were confirmed.

Not until the following month on 9th March, did Fan Bay Battery once more engage E-boats, when six rounds were fired but the results were not known. The first merchantman to be engaged was a vessel of some 800 tons on 10th April, and again 7 rounds from South Foreland fell in the target area, but no confirmation of the destruction of the vessel could be claimed. Twelve days later, a large tanker was engaged and 24 rounds from South Foreland were fired. From then on a number

A shell being manoeuvred into the breech of a long-range gun.

of engagements frequently took place and a number of hits on ships were recorded. Twelve small vessels certainly suffered seven hits, using 9.2 shrapnel and four hits, using A.P.C.

By 13th August, the 15 inch at Wanstone were ready, and the first record of their action was against two vessels about 1500 tons each, and they then fired 22 rounds, H.E. One vessel disappeared, obviously sunk, and the other was set on fire. South Foreland and Wanstone were now kept very busy. They had been instructed by the prime minister to keep the Strait closed to German shipping, and the gunners were doing their best to see that his orders were carried out. They did not engage the German guns, nor did they bombard the French ports of Calais and Boulogne. Ammunition was in short supply, and it was thought essential to make every round count. The 15 inch shells weigh about 2000 lbs., and were costly to fire, both in barrel wear and shell costing, so it was important that no round was wasted. The townsfolk often accused the local artillery of making holes in the French cliffs for sport, or just killing off a few Frenchmen in Calais and Boulogne as target practice. This was quite untrue. The soldiers were not permitted to reveal that the previous night they had engaged and sunk an important target, carrying valuable cargo, the enemy could ill afford to lose. The town suffered retaliatory shelling, and so some ill feeling naturally arose between the townspeople and the artillerymen, which was quite understandable. Every time the British guns fired, so the German guns ranged on Dover and more civilians were killed and more property destroyed. They stated in their ignorance at the time, that if the gunners had not been so trigger happy, then Dover would not have suffered another murderous onslaught. The only help the gunners could give, was a warning to the local police that they intended to open fire in about 30 minutes time, knowing that the result would be a shell attack on the town. The police sounded the shell warning, which consisted of two air raid warnings on the sirens with a short interval in between, to allow time for the local townspeople to seek shelter, many in local caves, before the first enemy shell arrived. It is worthy of note that even after a night's action, the batteries, next morning were in impeccable condition and ready for an inspection, due to the discipline, and energy of their commanding officer. This did much, not only to improve the efficiency of the batteries but also to improve the morale of all personnel. They considered themselves to be the kings of coast artillery. They were getting more action and more effective results, than any coast artillery in the world. They received more attention by political personalities and high ranking service officers, and they meant to keep it that way. They intended to ensure that the people of the town and port of Dover would remember these great guns, the work they did, and the destruction they caused in the Strait of Dover, for very many years to come.

And so the catalogue of their actions continued and is set out in greater detail in the appendix. One or two engagements are perhaps worthy of special note. Two large vessels of 1000 tons and 8000 tons were engaged on 12th August, 1942 with very effective result. The smaller vessel was undoubtedly sunk and the larger vessel crawled back to

Boulogne obviously heavily damaged. September 4th also saw the destruction of a 3000 ton vessel by South Foreland battery, 33 rounds fired, and Wanstone battery, 11 rounds fired. The radar echo of the vessel disappeared and the battle radar recorded seven direct hits and two probable hits. Two days later, a 4000 ton vessel, with two escorts, was engaged by both batteries and no less than fifteen hits and four probable hits were noted. Certainly at least one vessel was sunk, whilst the larger vessel turned back, badly damaged. The duration of the action was 48 minutes.

The following month on 9th November, another 4000 ton vessel, a merchantman, was without doubt destroyed off Cap Blanc Nez and the next day an even larger vessel, the 8900 ton armed raider *Neumark* was engaged and certainly hit a number of times and forced to take evasive action to escape. Hardly a week went by without the Germans trying desperately to run the gauntlet of our guns, often with dire results. On 5th July, 1943, they tried to rush two destroyers through the Strait. They were engaged by Wanstone, 20 rounds, and South Foreland, 40 rounds over a 52 minute period. Whilst the result cannot be confirmed, one vessel was seen to be on fire when it reached Calais, and a number of rounds were recorded on our radar in the target area.

On 4th September, yet another large vessel was engaged outside Calais, and set on fire. It certainly sank. On 2nd November, 1943, two enemy destroyers were engaged and some 20 rounds were fired by South Foreland and 18 rounds by Wanstone. No doubt they did effective damage as the battery radar recorded a number of hits, and a fire was observed on one destroyer. It was soon discovered that the enemy, having now located our guns and carefully noting the time of flight of our shells, and seen our gun flashes, would immediately alter the course and speed, to avoid being hit, which was no doubt a compliment to the accuracy of our fire. At first this manoeuvre proved successful and so it was decided to try and deceive the enemy. Another battery, Fan Bay and occasionally Langdon, were ordered to fire. Although these batteries had insufficient range to reach the enemy, their flashes were observed by the enemy vessel who would immediately take evasive action and would alter course and speed. As soon as the new course and speed was picked up by our radar, the heavier guns would open fire, a case of deception and counter deception.

One of the major engagements took place in the early hours of 20th January, 1944. Aerial reconnaisance had reported that a large vessel, believed to be carrying iron ore from Spain, was moored alongside the quay at Boulogne, and obviously preparing to make a dash through the straits, it being the darkest period of the month and the highest tide. It proved to be the 7000 ton vessel, the *Munsterland*. She was engaged by some 77 rounds from both batteries. The vessel was escorted by a number of smaller craft. She was hit off Cap Gris Nez and sank. Next morning, her superstructure was seen by the R.A.F. above the water, and a smaller vessel nearby was on fire. No effort was made by the Germans to remove the masts and funnels, sticking out of the water and so they provided a perfect datum point for our radar on the swept channel for some months

to come. The type of shell used by the South Foreland battery was invariably a special 8 C.R.H. and these were loaded manually, from a power driven hoist, requiring a long and exhaustive effort by the loading numbers. A rate of fire, averaging one round every 32 seconds was indeed a highly creditable performance, and whilst it put a heavy strain on the detachments, morale always remained high.

It was now obvious to all that the Dover guns had effectively carried out their mission to close the Strait, and any attempt to run the blockade would be extremely costly to the enemy.

The last action by the Dover guns took place in September, 1944. When Boulogne harbour was evacuated by enemy ships, a number were sunk. Then with the approval of the 1st Canadian Corps, who were now sweeping up the Pas de Calais, and the immediate fall of Boulogne became evident, the batteries were asked to give support, by engaging their old enemies in counter bombardment. The corps commander decided to use both Wanstone and the 14 inch Royal Marine Seige guns. On 16th September, fire was opened on Lindemann battery and the railway batteries near Wissant. 75 rounds were fired by Wanstone and 102 rounds by the Marines, resulting in a dozen direct hits on the batteries. The four guns on Cap Blanc Nez were shelled on 20th September by both Wanstone and the Marines, and six direct hits on the battery were recorded. During this period, the Germans heavily shelled Dover, but on 30th September, they were overrun by the Canadians, and so fired no more.

The Prime Minister inspecting a static mounted 15 inch naval gun at Wanstone Battery.

The Coast batteries and the Marines had done their work. Their barrels had been changed no fewer than four times, and this in itself had been a major operation, requiring the use of large railway lifting cranes, capable of lifting the 100 ton barrels. By now they were again worn out, so that their range became greatly reduced, but their job had been done and well done.

They had in fact carried out 62 actions against German shipping and 6 against the German batteries. They had sunk, with confirmation, no fewer than 26 ships. Wanstone had fired 1243 rounds and South Foreland 2248 rounds. The six inch batteries had fired 73 rounds. In addition, the Dover batteries had engaged a number of enemy aircraft and destroyed a number of flying bombs. Now that all threat of invasion had passed and the likelihood of the enemy being strong enough to make a serious raid, the guns of South Foreland and Wanstone followed the fate of the eight inch guns of Hougham and the six inch guns of Lydden Spout and Capel. They were put into what is termed in the army, a state of 'care and maintenance'. This simply meant that the stores were replaced, the ammunition returned to the magazines, and the working parts heavily greased. The guns and the sites remained, they were simply non-operational. Only the anti-motor torpedo boat battery of twin six pounders on the Eastern Arm and the three twelve pounders on the Pier Extension, remained in a high state of readiness.

This then had been our reply to the German threat to invade our country and to use our waters with impunity, a lesson we trust that any future invader or trespasser might do well to remember, although the means of repelling will no doubt have completely changed.

The former Lord Warden hotel, much loved by Victorian travellers, became HMS Wasp during the war as headquarters for controlling M.G.Bs., M.T.Bs. and Air Sea Rescue craft.

13 The cost

The defence of the town and port of Dover, through the most threatening period of its history, was now concluded, but not without considerable cost in lives and property.

Some 69 servicemen had been killed and over 100 seriously injured around the coast batteries, and several more had been washed over the side and drowned from the South Breakwater and Admiralty Pier, during severe weather in the winter months. Over 200 civilians had been killed and nearly 800 injured in Dover, whilst 457 houses had been destroyed and many thousands more had been damaged.

The local paper, the *Dover Express* published an excellent map of Dover, showing thereon the fall of shot of both shells and bombs, and it is difficult to find a single area in Dover unaffected by enemy action. It does not include the rounds which fell in the battery areas. The *Dover Express* goes on to record that no less than 2226 shells and 464 bombs and 3 parachute mines, fell on the town and the alert sounded no fewer than 3059 times.

When the European war ended, few indeed of the local territorials who had manned the defences of the town in 1939 remained. They were now serving in all the corners of the world. Their place had been taken by conscripted men, regulars from other units and later by their own townsfolk in the form of the Home Guard. A year or so after the war, however, another Territorial gunner regiment was formed, 410 Coast Regiment to train and man the guns and occupy the same seaward defence headquarters, as their wartime colleagues. Many men, who had served during the war, joined the new regiment, but its history, until it was finally disbanded and became a battalion of The Buffs in 1956 is another story.

To conclude the history of the Channel actions, and the defence of Dover, it is well to remember once again its vital strategic position as the Gateway of England, and whoever holds that gateway, it can truly be said to hold a knife at the throat of the whole country. The ghosts of the old gunners who manned the guns of the Lords Warden of the Cinque Ports, such men as Wellington and Pitt, who guarded the cliffs against an invader, might well feel some satisfaction in the manner the duties were discharged, when the need arose, and by the new generation. The weapons had changed, but the men were very much the same, with the

The Dover Express printed this map in its issue on 4th May, 1945.

156

DOVER'S SHELLS & BOMBS
1940 — 1944.

SHELLS ●   BOMBS ◐

Many more shells fell outside the
limits of this plan, which shows
the more thickly built-up area of
Dover.

Bombs	.. .. ..	464
Shells	.. ..	2,226
(12th Aug., 1940—26th Sept., 1944)		
Parachute Mines	.. ..	3
Alerts sounded	.. ..	3,059
(Air attacks	.. 2,872	
Shelling warnings	187)	
Civilian Deaths	.. ..	216
Severely injured	.. ..	344
Slightly „	.. ..	416
Premises damaged	..	10,056
Destroyed	957	
Severely damaged	2,914	

same problems and grievances, and the same wish to get the whole thing over as quickly as possible, so that they could resume their normal lives.

Dover would have to be rebuilt. Many of its old landmarks had disappeared or been reduced to rubble. No longer were the fine Regency houses of the seafront habitable. Some had been destroyed, most bore the scars of bombs and shells. The Guilford Lawn and Clarence Lawn had become a shambles, with the great Burlington Hotel in the rear, with its turret shot off, its windows blasted out, and gaping holes in its walls. Its counterpart, the Grand Hotel was in no better shape, having suffered a string of a bombs which also flattened the Granville Gardens and Camden Crescent. Many of the ancient and narrow streets and lanes, once the haunts of smugglers and seamen from Admiral Nelson's ships, had gone. The old Snargate Street, in the nineteenth century, the centre of the shopping district, with its quaint old shops, ship's chandlers, Wellington Cinema, and Hippodrome, famed all over the country, and old pubs, the haunt of mariners, from the ships in the Granville and Wellington docks, had been blasted almost beyond recognition. Today it is difficult even to find the sites of some of these old buildings, or to imagine how the area looked before the war. The building of great roads to accommodate the heavy continental traffic, have swept away the Liverpool Street Drill Hall, the former home of the local Territorials, and a vast new road has been run up the side of the cliffs on to the Northfall Meadow, to speed the T.I.R. lorries on their way, and avoid the town of Dover. Where knights in armour from the Castle once jousted for a lady's favour, now the same ground rumbles with the tread of heavy lorries.

Hovercraft and similar landing grounds now rise over the sea and pier, where once the *Great Harry* swung at anchor, and docks and ferry berths have swamped the ancient batteries and berths of ships, which not so very long ago provided protection for vessels using the port for trade.

The defences which have already been described, have also disappeared. The batteries each side of the tidal harbour and guarding the entrance to the basin and pents, have been overrun by warehouses, dock sheds and the like. The great 81 tonners of the Admiralty Pier, too heavy to be removed, have been boarded over, and a pedestrian shelter now rests where the six inch guns of both world wars, guarded the approaches from the west. The gun sites on the Western Cliffs, Drop Redoubt, Archcliffe, Western Redoubt and beyond, have all gone, although the gun houses of the Western Heights battery, stripped of their six inch guns, and gaping like some toothless old man, can still be seen, overlooking the harbour. All the batteries on the harbour moles have been removed and also the battery observation towers, controlling them. The concrete barrack rooms on the Southern Breakwater, stand empty and shabby with windows barred and doors bolted. As I gazed despairingly on the remains of the old guard room, at the head of the stone steps, up the side of the Breakwater, the guard room in which we took such pride in fortifying against an attack along the Breakwater, I was accosted by a man wearing a cap, bearing the insignia 'Dover Harbour Board'. He demanded that I pay the sum of 10p. for the

The shell of the Hippodrome remained standing among the wreckage of Snargate Street and Northampton Street while an exchange of land there for the sea front enabled the building of the Gateway flats by Dover Borough Council and more dock installations by the Harbour Board.

privilege of being there. How ironic, I thought, as I paid my toll. Forty years ago, things would have been a lot different. I remember when I walked up those very same steps, to take command of two 6 inch guns and one twin 6 pounder, five officers and 140 men, all in spick and span condition.

Langdon Battery presented an even more dismal and depressing picture. The concrete gun sites were still there but the remainder of the battery presented a picture of ruin and neglect. Most of the huts had collapsed, windows of the more permanent buildings were broken and doors hanging down, broken from their hinges. Paint had peeled off and everywhere there was ruin and decay. Far better to have utterly destroyed this once proud battery, which had served in two world wars, than leave it to defacement by vandals. The old gun, formerly a holdfast, which I had dug up at the rear of the battery, still stands where I had left it, but now overgrown with grass and weed. The Langdon Barracks, once the smart store and equipment area, has completely changed its identity. Gone is the great Victorian gateway entrance, gone is the great long high brick wall, once the prison surround, gone are the smart buildings containing the ration store, the medical inspection room, the Q.M. stores and offices. It was a place I hardly recognised. As I entered I was greeted by a kiosk selling ice cream! The entrance to the tunnel, leading down through the cliffs to Eastern Arm was difficult to discover, being now hidden in a mass of brambles and blackberry bushes. The levels are still there, and they are now the habitat of hosts of motorists, who park

Above
*The Gateway flats
were built by Dover
Borough Council on
the sea front in the
late 1950's after
much local
argument.*
Opposite
*Aerial view of Dover
sea front area after
the war. Note
Burlington Hotel in
the centre and the
Grand Hotel on left.*

their cars, facing the sea and enjoy watching the activities in the Eastern Docks, and shipping in the channel, little knowing that where they now stand, once stood convicts and French prisoners of war, looking toward the French cliffs, clearly to be seen on a fine day. I did however find the old concrete base, used in my gun shifting exercise with the six inch gun. It is now partly overgrown, but the rusted holdfast bolts are still there, and they are now objects of curiosity and speculation by the motorists who happen to park nearby.

The batteries of Wanstone and South Foreland, whose role had been offensive as opposed to the harbour defensive guns, have practically disappeared. Although the concrete gun pits remain, and evidence of the plotting rooms and power house, there is very little else. The land has been returned to the farmer who has made good use of it. Little if anything remains of Fan Bay, and Lydden Spout, Hougham or Capel. A few concrete bunkers, all overgrown and derelict, and it would be a kindness to remove even these ruins. Citadel battery is now within the confines of the present day Borstal Institution and, I have no doubt, more comfortable today than in the days when it was used by the local militia. The Royal Marine guns, Winnie and Pooh, impeded the members of the Kingsdown Golf Course, so had to be removed speedily. Likewise the other guns, one in fact named Bruce was never fired in anger. It is said that Winnie and Pooh were dismantled and sent abroad for the war against the Japanese.

And so a great era has passed into obscurity. Means of destruction have become far more scientific. Man can destroy themselves at far greater ranges and with far less effort. The defence of the realm no longer lies in the hands of the coast artillery and garrison artillery. These have passed into history, just as their forebears did in the old days of the bow and arrow. Dover still grows in area and industry. It is still the Gateway to England, whether it is more prosperous than in the days of yore, it is impossible to say. Frankly I doubt it. Dovorians still provide men, like any other town or city, for the services, but no local volunteer now mans any defences around the town because there are none. Neither is the town required to supply men and ships for the Royal Navy as the old law of the Cinque Ports once demanded. Many things have changed in the interests of progress and the advance of civilisation to a better world. Or is it?

Let us finish this narrative with the words of Sir Walter Raleigh. 'Dover is so well suited to annoying the enemy, protecting commerce, or the sending and receiving of dispatches.' Sir Winston Churchill, however, in a more expansive mood stated that we were 'exposing ourselves to what might be a vexatious affront should we allow, at any time, the Germans to seize even a part of Dover and hold it for a short period.'

What better conclusion to *Conflict across the Strait* than the words of two wise and famous Englishmen.

Above
Their job completed, the guns were broken up and the White Cliffs of Dover returned to peace again.
Right, top
Some members of 'P' Battery of the new 410 Coast Regiment of R.A.T.A., winners of the Emden Trophy, with their twin six-pounder in the Liverpool Street Drill Hall after the war.
Right, bottom
'P' Battery with 9·2 inch gun at Pendennis Castle, Falmouth, in 1952.

APPENDIX I

A record of the actions of the 540 Coast Regiment R.A. against enemy shipping in the Dover Strait.

Date	Target	Rounds Fired	Batteries Used	Results	Duration	Remarks
1942 Feb 6th	E-Boats	15 — 6 in	Fan Bay	N/K	20 mins	Controlled by C.A. Operations Room
Feb 12th	*Scharnhorst Gneisnau Prinz Eugen*	33 — 9.2 APC	South Foreland	3 hits confirmed	17 mins	Controlled by Fire Commander
Mar 9th	E-Boats	6 — 6 in	Fan Bay	N/K	13 mins	Controlled by C.A. Operations Room
Apr 10th	Merchant Vessel 800 tons	7 — 9.2 HE	South Foreland	Unobserved and minus	17 mins	No definite drill
Apr 22nd	Large tanker	24 — 9.2 APC	South Foreland	6 O/U. 2 minus	17 mins	F.C. controlled direct to BPR
Jun 22nd	Four Trawlers	8 — 9.2 HE	South Foreland	O/U	7 mins	Fortress Plotter
Jul 2nd	Twelve small Vessels	4 — 9.2 HE & 80 — 9.2 APC	South Foreland	4 probable K.K. 7 K.K.	28 mins	First full action communications and drill
Jul 8th	Vessel 1000 tons and escort	33 — 9.2	South Foreland	5 K.K. Vessel took avoiding action	22 mins	Enemy shelled batteries
Aug 13th	2 Vessels 1500 tons	22 — 15 in 36 — 9.2 HE 8 CRH 18 — 9.2 HE	Wanstone South Foreland	1 O.K. 6 K.K.	51 mins	One vessel disappeared
Aug 14th	1 vessel 4000 tons and escorts	43 — 15 in HE 58 — 9.2 HE 8 CRH 18 — 9.2 HE	Wanstone South Foreland	19 K.K.	69 mins	Enemy changing tactics to line abreast

Date	Target details	Guns (CPBC)	Battery	Result	Time	Outcome
Aug 17th	2 large vessels 8000 & 1000 tons	25 — 15 in	Wanstone	Large vessel turned back 6 K.K.	51 mins	Procedure A
Aug 24th	Small craft	6 — 6 in	Fan Bay	Not known	12 mins	Procedure B
Sept 4th	1 vessel 3000 tons	11 — 15 in 33 — 9.2 HE 8 CRH	Wanstone South Foreland	2 probable O.K. 7 K.K.	28 mins	One vessel disappeared
Sept 6th	1 vessel 4000 tons and escorts	34 — 15 in HE 68 — 9.2 HE 8 CRH	Wanstone South Foreland	4 probable O.K. 15 K.K.	48 mins	One vessel disappeared large vessel believed damaged
Nov 9th	1 vessel 4000 tons 4 escorts	24 — 15 in HE 140 — 9.2 8 CRH	Wanstone South Foreland	1 O.K. 19 K.K.	99 mins	Target sunk
Nov 10th	Armed raider *Neumark* 8000 tons	25 — 15 in HE 34 — 9.2 in 8 CRH	Wanstone South Foreland	4 K.K.	55 mins	Target took strong evasive action
Dec 10th	Sperrbrecher 2000 tons with escorts	36 — 15 in 8 CRH	Wanstone	11 K.K.	52 mins	Prisoners report targets hit by splinters Salvoes fell very near
1943 Jan 20th	Not known	14 — 6 in HE	Fan Bay	Not known		Procedure B
Feb 9th	1 vessel 500 ton 2 smaller vessels	11 — 6 in	Fan Bay	Wreck found next morning off Calais		Procedure B

Date	Target	Rounds Fired	Batteries Used	Results	Duration	Remarks
Feb 10th	Merchantman 5/6000 tons with 2 escorts	33—15 in HE 93—9.2 HE 8 CRH	Wanstone South Foreland	Not known		Hostile counter battery fire very heavy
Feb 14th	3 large vessels and 2 small vessels	13—15 in 45—9.2 8 CRH	Wanstone South Foreland	One vessel seen to be on fire		Hostile counter battery fire very heavy
Mar 2nd	1 large vessel and 2 smaller vessels	177—9.2 HE 8 CRH	South Foreland	5 hits		Target brought to standstill Navy report target disappeared BPR hit and put out of action
Mar 12th	1 large vessel 1 medium and several small	38—15 in HE 73—9.2 HE 8 CRH	South Foreland	2 probable and 3 straddles	74 mins	RAF report target sunk
Apr 5	1 large merchantman 390 ft and 1 vessel 1000 tons with escorts	72—15 in HE 15—9.2 HE 8 CRH	Wanstone South Foreland	13 probable hits 12 straddles	106 mins	Large vessel damaged 1000 ton vessel sunk
May 1st	1 vessel 350 ft and 4 escorts	50—15 in HE 12—9.2 HE 8 CRH	Wanstone South Foreland	4 hits	56 mins	Large vessel damaged
Jun 28th	Large convoy 1 large vessel 1 medium vessel number of escorts	14—15 in HE 38—9.2 in HE 8 CRH	Wanstone South Foreland	1 hit	52 mins	Seen by HM ships
Jul 5th	2 destroyers	20—15 in HE 40—9.2 in HE 8 CRH	Wanstone South Foreland	Number of rounds in target area	52 mins	N/K
Sept 2nd	4 trawler	40—9.2 in	Wanstone	Shots in target area	21 mins	N/K

Date	Target	Ammunition	Battery	Result	Time	
Sept ...	1 medium vessel 6 escorts	HE 8 CRH 4 – 15 in APC	... South Foreland	Large vessel sunk Medium vessel on fire outside Calais	To mins	
Oct 3rd	1 medium vessel	15 – 15 in APC 68 – 9.2 in 8 CRH	Wanstone South Foreland	Vessel took violent evasive action	49 mins	
Oct 4th	1 medium vessel 350 feet approx 8 escorts	35 – 15 in HE & APC 56 – 9.2 in HE 8 CRH	Wanstone South Foreland	Large vessel sunk. 1 escort beached near Cap Gris Nez Trawler also beached	40 mins	
Oct 25th	1 medium vessel 350 ft approx 5 escorts	42 – 15 in (15 super chgd) 6 CRH & APC 12 – 9.2 HE 8 CRH 12 – 6 in Practice shot	Wanstone South Foreland Fan Bay	R-Boat sunk Large vessel sunk	104 mins	
Nov 3rd	2 destroyers	18 – 15 in HE super chrgd 20 – 9.2 HE 8 CRH 12 – 6 in Practice shot	Wanstone South Foreland Fan Bay	2 straddles Fire Observed aboard destroyer	33 mins	N/K
Dec 4th	1 destroyer 6/8 escorts	10 – 15 in 4 CRH super chrgd 34 – 9.2 HE 8 CRH 30 – 6 in P/S	Wanstone South Foreland Fan Bay	One straddle	18 mins	N/K
Dec 23rd	1 large tanker 15 escorts	52 – 15 in 4 CRH super chrgd 26 – 9.2 in 8 CRH	Wanstone South Foreland	Five straddles	66 mins	N/K

This regrettably is as far as the records go and further action by the 540 Coast Regiment is not available.

A summary of the story of Wanstone and South Foreland, extracted from the Regimental diary, 540 Coast Regiment R.A.

1942
The Real Task.
The 'Gun Duel' fallacy.
The Targets.
How it was done.
The Operations Room.
The *Scharnhorst* and *Gnisenau.* South Foreland alone.
Wanstone joins in.
Four merchantmen.
Combined operations — the *Neumark.*
More merchantmen.
1942 Reviewed.

1943
Mostly merchantmen.
First success — the iron-ore carrier.
Naval co-operation.
Avoiding tactics — some hits.
R.A.F. co-operation.
Two destroyers — another combined operation.
Probable success — The *Lothringen.*
Two actions in one night.
Convoy hit and dispersed.
More combined operations.
Two more destroyers.
An unfamiliar target the *Ostfriesland.*
1943 in retrospect.

1944
The sinking of the *S.S. Munsterland.*
Destroyers or Sperrbrechers.
Three Sperrbrechers.
Three targets in three nights.
The sinking of the tanker *S.S. Rekum.*
Two more tankers.
D-Day and after.
The evacuation of Boulogne.
The first battle.
'Gun Duels' at last.
The last battle.
The tactical role.

Confirmation of 26 ships sunk and a total of 3491 rounds fired.

Glossary

LIST OF ABBREVIATIONS AND TERMS

A.A. – Anti-aircraft or ack-ack.

A.M.T.B. – Anti-motor topedo boat.

A.P.B.C. or A.P.C. – Armour piercing shell (ballistic cap).

A.R.P. – Air raid precautions.

A.T.S. – (Women's) Auxiliary Territorial Service.

Autosight – Telescopic system of range finding.

B.C. – Battery Commander.

B.C.A. – Battery Commander's Assistant, records all orders and observation of shot by B.C.

B.D.O. – Boom Defence Officer, R.N., controls opening and closing of a boom across a defended area.

B.L. – Breech-loading gun.

B.O.P – Battery observation post from which fire is directed by B.C.

B.P.R. – Battery plotting room from which information regarding the range, bearing, course and speed of target is ultimately received and whence ranges and bearings are suitably corrected and passed to the guns.

B.S.M. – Battery Sergeant Major.

Case II & Case III – Systems of range finding.

C.A.S.L. – Coast artillery searchlights.

C.C.C.A. – Corps Commander Coast Artillery.

C.C.R.A. – Corps Commander Royal Artillery.

C.H.L. – Chain home low, radar station built to watch for low level 'sneak raids' by enemy fighter bombers.

C.I.G.S. – Chief of the Imperial General Staff.

C.O. – Commanding Officer.

C.P. – Command Post.

C.R.H. – Calibre radius head, measurement at the cap or nose of a shell.

Datum – A system whereby the accuracy of the bearing and range on instruments are tested. Adjustments are necessary for rise and fall of tide, variation of refraction and gun usage, etc.

D.P.F. – Depression position finder. Tracks target on a gridded chart, measures bearings and ranges from the gun for which it is set up. Automatically transmits to dials set up on the gun mountings.

D.R.F. – Depression range finder. An optical instrument measuring ranges and bearings up to 12,000 yards.

E.D.O. – Extended Defence Officer (R.N.).

F.C. – Fire Commander. Officer in charge of fire command covering a defended area.

F.C.P. – Fire Commander's post from which F.C. operates.

F.O.P. – One of a chain of selected positions from which the enemy may be observed and sometimes his position is plotted.

G.O.C. – General Officer Commanding.

G.P.O. – Gun Position Officer. Officer at the guns responsible for the correct transmission of the B.C.'s orders.

H.E. – High explosive.

H.V.F.C. – High velocity full charge.

Ladder – A system of ranging.

L.M.G. – Lewis machine guns.

Magslip – An electrical system of transmitting ranges and bearings from any type of range-finding instrument to gun mounting.

M.G.B. – Motor gun boat.

M.T.B. – Motor torpedo boat.

N.C.O. – Non-Commissioned Officer.

P.A.D. – Passive Air defence.

P.R.U. – Patrol reconnaissance unit.

P.S.I. – Permanent staff instructor.

P.W.S.S. – Port war signal station (R.N.). Transmits all signals and challenges to naval and all other types of vessel approaching the port.

Q.F. – Quick-firing gun.

R.A. – Royal Artillery.

R.A.F. – Royal Air Force.

R.A.T.A. – Royal Artillery Territorial Army.

R.B.L. – Rifled breech-loading gun.

R.E. – Royal Engineers.

R.G.A. – Royal Garrison Artillery.

R.H.Q. – Regimental headquarters.

R.Q.M.S. – Regimental Quarter Master Sergeant.

R.M.L. – Rifled muzzle-loading gun. The projectile is loaded from the front or nose of the gun.

R.N. – Royal Navy.

R.N.V.R. – Royal Navy Volunteer Reserve.

R.S.M. – Regimental Sergeant Major.

Salvo Fire – A method of fire. Guns are fired simultaneously on the orders of the G.P.O., the intervals of salvoes being indicated by the B.C.

U.P. – Unrotated (unrifled) projectile.

V.I.P. – Very important person.

W.O. – Warrant Officer.

X.D.O. – Extended Defence Officer (R.N.). Located in the F.C. post. Advises F.C. on the identity of all naval vessels, also operates controlled mine-fields at the entrances of a defended area.

X.V. – Examination vessel.

ACKNOWLEDGEMENTS

The author gratefully acknowledges the help, information and advice he has received during the writing of this book, in particular from the military historian Ian V. Hogg, Dave Collyer and John Guy, members of Kent Defence Research Group, Mrs. B. Raw, Mrs. B. Crellin, Mrs. D. Sloggett, Brigadier J. H. W. G. Richards, OBE, DL, Lt.-Comdr. C. E. Vidler, MBE, Cyril Brown, Harold Sneller, Bob Hollingsbee, Mike Pascall, Trevor Hocking, Nigel Smith, the editor of the Dover Express, Dover Harbour Board, Mr. J. S. Lucas, and the staff of Dover Public Library. To Doug Welby without whose untiring efforts, enthusiasm and inspiration this work would never have been published.

As many of the illustrations are copies of originals, whose pedigree is somewhat obscure, it would therefore be an impossible task to trace all the copyright holders. The author would therefore like to thank any whom he has been unable to list below and he expresses regret for their omission.

ILLUSTRATIONS

Photographs and illustrations have been supplied, or are reproduced, by kind permission of the following organizations.

Imperial War museum: p. 32, 67, 73, 121, 123, 124, 129, 131, 144, 148, 150, 154, 155.

Dover Harbour Board: p. 24, 25, 45, 46, 71.

Dover Express: p. 92, 157.

South Eastern Newspapers Ltd. [Kent Messenger]: p. 119, 136/137, 139.

Dover Museum: p. 6, 14, 18, 159.

Dover Library: p. 13, 17, 31.

List of Illustrations

Index

SILHOUETTES OF SOME BRITISH VESSELS

"CHEQUERS" CLASS DESTROYER ($362\frac{3}{4}$' X $35\frac{2}{3}$')

"BLACK SWAN" CLASS A/A FRIGATE ($299\frac{1}{2}$' X $38\frac{1}{2}$')

"CASTLE" CLASS FRIGATE (252' X $36\frac{2}{3}$')

"ALGERINE" CLASS OCEAN SWEEPER (225' X $35\frac{1}{2}$')

"ISLES" CLASS TRAWLER (164' X $27\frac{2}{3}$')

"FORD CLASS SEAWARD DEFENCE BOAT (117' X 20')

X CRAFT SMALL ATTACK CRAFT ($53\frac{1}{6}$' X $5\frac{5}{6}$')

S.D.M.L. CLASS SEAWARD DEFENCE CRAFT (72' X $15\frac{5}{6}$')

M.F.V. MOTOR FISHING VESSEL (75' X 12')

"HAM" CLASS INSHORE MINESWEEPER ($106\frac{1}{2}$' X $21\frac{1}{6}$')

F.P.B. FAST PATROL BOAT ($122\frac{2}{3}$' X 20')

"MINER" CLASS MINELAYING LIGHTER ($118\frac{1}{2}$' X $26\frac{1}{2}$')

"CONISTON" CLASS COASTAL SWEEPER (152' X 28')